God, the Bible and Common Sense
Copyright 1978 by Leroy Brownlow

ISBN 0-915720-48-5

Brownlow Publishing Company, Incorporated
6309 Airport Freeway, Fort Worth, Texas 76117

LEROY BROWNLOW

BROWNLOW PUBLISHING COMPANY, INC.
FORT WORTH, TEXAS

Contents

Chapter	Page
I. Common Sense Requires God	7
II. The Common Sense Biblical Account of Creation	17
III. That God Created Man Makes Sense	24
IV. Christ's Coming to Earth Makes Sense	37
V. Common Sense Demands The Bible	47
VI. Common Sense Requires Right Division of Bible	57
VII. The Church Makes Sense	68
VIII. God's Plan of Salvation Is Sensible	78
IX. The Common Sense of Christian Growth	88
X. Worship Is Sensible	97
XI. Common Sense at Random in the Scriptures	106
XII. God's Appointment of Death Is Sensible	115
XIII. The Judgment Makes Sense	124

Foreword

THE purpose of this book is to place before mankind the common sense of the reality of God and of His work and of His religion for man.

— *Leroy Brownlow*

I
Common Sense Requires God

THE writer of Hebrews appeals to common sense to prove the existence of God. He said:

> For every house is builded by some man; but he that built all things is God.
> — Hebrews 3:4

Now that makes sense. No house can build itself. Neither could a world accidentally have happened. To say that either could have created itself is monstrously unscientific and grossly nonsensical. Any created thing requires a creator. Every effect must have a cause. So science and sanity are on the side of God — the Creator, the First Cause.

Neither globes nor worlds just happen. It is reputed that the famous infidel Robert Ingersoll, while visiting a friend, picked up a globe and asked, "Who made this?" "Nobody, it just made itself," replied the believer. Absurd! Ridiculous! Yet infidels would have us to believe that they belong to a class of keen-minded, perceptive intellectuals. In fact, they have rolled their no-God band wagon on college campuses and exhorted youth to hop on if they wish to be known as smart and progressive people. Nevertheless, holding to the idea that a house or a world built itself is not brilliant.

Thus the Bible repeatedly presents to man the only explanation of creation — that God created it.

> In the beginning God created the heaven and the earth.
> — Genesis 1:1

8 God, the Bible and Common Sense

> Thus saith God the Lord, he that created the heavens, and stretched them out; he that spread forth the earth, and that which cometh out of it; he that giveth breath unto the people upon it, and spirit to them that walk therein.
> —Isaiah 42:5

> All things have been created through him, and unto him.
> — Colossians 3:16

A SELF-EXISTENT FIRST CAUSE

1. *There is no explanation of creation apart from a self-existent First Cause.* Absolutely none! Some Being or something had to be self-existent in the beginning from which everything else has come. This is most evident! Note this syllogism:

> Something cannot come from nothing (unquestionable).
> But something is (does exist).
> Therefore, something always was.

Even the atheist agrees with the believer that something cannot come from nothing. And since something is, then something has always been. That something is either lifeless matter or a Being (God).

Who or what was it? The very first words in the Bible tell us that it was God (Gen. 1:1). For this kind of reasoning (that an effect must have a cause) to be in the Bible is surely shocking to the atheist. And this is only the first sentence in it.

2. *Since there has to be a beginning point, which idea is more reasonable: begin with self-existent dead matter or begin with self-existent powerful Life?* The atheist tries to account for the world through an evolutionary process in which he retrogresses step by step until he finally gets back to a minute speck of lifeless, powerless matter. Ask him where this came from and

he admits he does not know; there his speculations fail; there he stands enveloped in gross confusion; there his whole theory raises many questions in its defiance of rationality, of which we ask him, as follows:

(1) Since we have to begin with the self-existence of something or some Being, why do you choose to begin with dead matter in preference to all-powerful Life?

(2) Why do you think it would be easier for matter to be self-existent than for God to be self-existent? When you speak of matter, you speak of that which belongs to strict and lifeless limitations, to restrictions where it is irrational to think that a material substance could ever be self-existent. But the thought of God transcends human weaknesses and puts us in an entirely different field — the supernatural — where nothing is impossible and inexplainable, and accordingly makes it plausible for Him to be the self-existent First Cause.

In a recent debate, 1976, between an atheist and a Christian, the atheist spoke for some ten or fifteen minutes in one session, contending that there are things which cannot be explained. He thereby unwittingly conceded his position because everything can be explained in the natural world. If there are things that cannot be explained, then there is the Supernatural — a power beyond nature — which means God. He talked and talked, not knowing he was arguing our side.

(3) If dead matter were the moving force behind creation, how did it — unaffected by any other source — get moving? For there would have been absolutely nothing to act upon it. Now this is a pertinent question; for it is evident that if a force could move through its own power, it would not be dead matter but life. Matter has never been able to move of its own accord. It remains stationary until an outside force acts upon it. Therefore, all motion presupposes the existence of Mind as it operates

on matter. Consequently, a common-sense conclusion is that God was the First Cause and not matter.

(4) For dead matter to become a moving force, it would have to get alive; so we ask: *How did it get alive? How did it become all-powerful?* The atheist has no answers. If the dead matter were from everlasting to everlasting, and became alive, and omnipotent, and omnific, then the atheist would have a *god,* the very thing he refuses to accept. So his own illogical thinking traps him in his own dilemma. How much more sensible it is to accept God as the self-existent First Cause and start from there.

3. *It is unscientific to presume that life sprang from no life.* Jordan and Kellogg in their book, *Evolution and Animal Life,* p. 41, make this statement:

> All life comes from life. The biologist cannot admit spontaneous generation in the face of the scientific evidence he has.

There is no *scientific* way to account for life without a beginning Life.

The person who rejects God as creator is caught in a predicament similar to that of the crated dog in the Railway Express Office. A gentleman in the office said to the manager, "Where is that dog going?" The manager, thoroughly disgusted, said, "I don't know. You don't know. He don't know. Nobody don't know! Because he has already gone and chawed up his tag." That describes the atheist. He has "chawed" up his tag. He does not know from whence he came, why he is here, or where he is going. And that is not smart.

EVIDENCE IN THE SKY

1. *The universe is a big bulletin board which carries the sensible declaration — G-O-D.* Truly —

> The heavens declare the glory of God; and the firmament showeth his handiwork.
>
> — Psalms 19:1

Unequivocally, there is no way to account for the number and order of the celestial bodies except in terms of supernaturalness.

2. *The number of stars and the immensity of space are staggering.* With the aid of a high-powered telescope 100,000,000 stars are visible on a clear night. Photographic plates reveal hundreds of millions more. Scientists say beyond these are countless numbers of planets and stars we have never been able to see. The immensity of space goes on and on (and if space can go on and on, so can eternity). Scientists say that some stars are as far as one hundred quadrillion miles away. What power brought all this space and all these stars into existence? The discerning answer is found in the lesson text: "For every house is built by some man; but he that built all things is God" (Heb. 3:4).

3. *Throughout creation there is design.* The stars are not hanging at random but are grouped together in numberless universes. If God did not design and group them then who or what did?

To say that they are an accident is just as silly as to say that the Fort Worth Telephone Directory is the result of an explosion in a printing plant.

It has been calculated that if the twenty-six letters of the alphabet were tossed together into the air by chance, they might fall together in their regular order — A,B,C, through X,Y,Z — once in five hundred million, million, million times. With this as a basis, what would be the probability of the millions of stars — not just twenty-six — creating themselves and coming together through accident and blind chance? This pertinent question needs an answer.

Years ago an infidel said to a French peasant, "We will pull down your churches. We will destroy everything that reminds you of God." The peasant cleverly and confidently replied, "But you will leave us the sun, the moon, and the stars, and as long as they shine we shall have a reminder of God."

GRAVITATION

1. *Gravitation is a force which moves our earth rapidly and systematically* so that days and nights and seasons come in regular order. This same force moves all the planets in such perfect precision that astronomers can correctly predict an eclipse a hundred years from now. Who or what was the lawmaker that gave the law of gravitation? "Nobody! Nothing! It just happened!" the disbeliever says. Nonsense! For every law requires a lawmaker.

2. Inasmuch as this law is beyond humanity, then *its origin and continuance must rest in the Superhuman — God*. The Bible attributes this force to Him: "But the heavens and the earth, which are now, by the same word are kept in store" (II Pet. 3:7). Reject this and there is no explanation.

ARGUMENTS EXAMINED

1. *The atheist insists that God is not real, that man's own internal need caused him to invent God.* Isn't that strange? Because man's internal urgency is one of our arguments to prove God's reality. No nation or tribe has ever been discovered that does not practice some form of religion. Man's longing for God proves that he has a spirit that craves communion with the Great Spirit and assistance from Him. This is the Biblical exposition: "That they should seek the Lord, if haply they might feel after him, and find him, though he be not far from every one of us" (Acts 17:27).

Our ignorance is so widespread; our questions so numerous; our sins so infamous; our frailty so weak; our burdens so heavy; and our desire for immortality so deep. All of this emphasizes man's inner nature, that there is something within him that cries out for help. Now let us reason: Shall we seek the solution to our problems by closing our eyes to their existence? Shall we muffle these cries of the soul by denying that we hear the cries or that we have souls? Shall we answer the eternal longing of man for companionship with God by denying that He exists? By ridiculing His reality? By making sport of life? Can we find fulness of life in such an easy manner?

No! Disbelief does not satisfy. Simply because man is the offspring of God, made in His image. And most confirmed disbelievers sooner or later come to that place in life where they feel as Robert G. Ingersoll felt, standing by the tomb of his brother, who spoke of "a short, barren space between two cold, bleak points of eternity." Then it is that they "strive in vain to look beyond." Then it is that even in the infidel heart, as Ingersoll stated, "hope sees a star, and listening, love hears the rustle of a wing."

2. A favorite rejoinder is: "If God is real and religion came from Him (not invented by man), then *why do we have so many different religions?*" This does not verify that man invented religion but rather that he has corrupted it. Their common resemblances prove that they came from a common source and that a pure one. All erroneous religions are but perversions of God's original revelation to man. What happened is explained in Eccl. 7:29: "God hath made man upright; but they have sought out many inventions."

3. *Some say, "I won't believe in a God I cannot see."* How inconsistent! For they believe in many other things they cannot see. They cannot see pain — only its effects. Love and hate are not visible — only their fruits. Neither can electricity be

seen — only the results — and by just looking, no man can tell a hot wire from a cold one. So it is rational to believe in a thing you cannot see, including God. If God could be seen with the material eye, He would not be Spirit and thus not God; for if He had the material qualities that are visible, He could not be omnipresent.

4. *Some rebound, "I will not believe in a God who cannot be proved by science."* He was here first. We need God to prove science — not science to prove God. He is too big to put in a test tube. Too big for man's little laboratory. Don't make the mistake of wanting a God no bigger than a man. The mistake of the centuries is aptly expressed in Psalms 50:21: "Thou thoughtest that I was altogether such a one as thyself."

5. *Others argue, "If there is a God, why does He permit war?"* Because He has given man volition. This freedom allows a man to knock another man down. Multiply this a million times and you have a world war. Of course, it is a misuse of human freedom, but nobody wants man's free will removed because he may ill-treat it. Remember — common sense tells us that we cannot have it both ways. So let us not ask God to take the rap for man's perversion of freedom.

6. *"If there is a God, why did he give death?" inquire others.* This, too, is common sense. See Chapter XII.

CONCLUDING THOUGHTS

1. *Any person can doubt anything,* but remember — that does not alter its reality nor the consequences of the act.

2. *This is the story of humanity:* some "worshipped him: but some doubted" (Matt. 28:17). However, the evidence was the same to both.

3. *An underlying reason for atheism is self-centeredness*

— not a lack of evidence. Infidelity is not due to insufficient proof but to a person's internal condition — blinded eyes and hardened heart (Matt. 13:15). The hidden, selfish desire to run the show, to call the plays — yes, one's urge to be his own little god — may cause him to reject the true and living God; and in the compounding process he finds it more comfortable to refuse God by denying that He exists. Rebellion is often the seat of unbelief.

4. *The person who rejects God in infidelity* turns from Him whose name has stood the abuses and distortions of would-be friends and the oppositions and railings of admitted enemies. Yet God is as real and merciful as ever (Neh. 9:16,17). He turns from Him whose love has lifted the most sinful from the lowest depths of degradation to the highest heights of exemplary goodness; he rejects the God who offers to take from man's cup the dregs of sorrow and to refill it with the draught of happiness. In this disbelief, he sets himself afloat in a rudderless, leaky boat of human wisdom upon an uncharted, stormy sea with no pilot to guide and no hope to beckon. This makes no sense!

REVIEW EXERCISE

1. What illustration is given in the book of Hebrews that shows the world could not have created itself? ....
   ....

2. Give the syllogism which proves there was a self-existent First Cause. ....

3. What do the heavens declare? ....
   ....

4. From a mathematical viewpoint, what likelihood is there that the universe accidentally came into order? ....
....

5. What did Peter say is the force that keeps the universe in running order? ....

6. What are the problems the atheist has when he uses dead matter as the beginning of everything? ....
....

7. Answer: "I won't believe in a God I cannot see." ....
....

8. Answer: "If there is a God, why does He permit war?" ....
....

9. (T or F) Many make the mistake of wanting a God no bigger than man. Scripture: ....

10. Thought for discussion: Since we have to begin with the self-existence of something, it is easier for God to be self-existent than for matter to be self-existent.

11. Thought for discussion: The underlying reason for atheism is self-centeredness.

12. Thought for discussion: Disbelief cannot satisfy the longings of man.

II

The Common Sense Biblical Account of Creation

TRUTH never contradicts itself. Any supposed contradiction between the Bible and science is due to a lack of understanding of either one or the other or maybe both.

The Bible speaks of "science falsely so called" (I Tim. 6:20), and it also reproves false interpretations of the Bible. Both are possibilities. A scientist can hold a scientific theory which is not science at all — just a view of it. Likewise, a preacher can hold an interpretation of the Bible that is not Bible at all — just an opinion of it. Admittedly, preachers have at times displayed their unenlightenment of both the Bible and science, but no more than scientists. The scientists have changed their views from year to year, so much that any text book ten years old is considered obsolete. However, in all fairness, we hasten to say that some scientists believe in God and His creative power. To read of the convictions of a few of the many, see *Scientists Who Believe,* 1963, published by David C. Cook Publishing Co., Elgin, Illinois.

While the Bible is a textbook on the science of right living instead of material sciences, yet we contend that any statement incidentally made on any of the other sciences is accurate. "For the word of the Lord is right" (Psa. 33:4).

THE BIBLICAL RECORD OF THE WORLD'S ORIGIN

1. *The Bible says there was a beginning:* "In the beginning" (Gen. 1:1). This is absolutely scientific. Completely sensible.

The science of radioactivity says that material things have a beginning and should have an ending. This is known from the study of properties which give off "rays which consist either of electrified particles (alpha and beta rays) or of radiant energy of high frequency (gamma rays)." The giving off of energy which cannot be put back is proof there had to be a beginning. The slow cooling of the sun is a common example.

The Genesis record that there was a beginning, a setting in order and a winding up is supported by the science of thermodynamics, which states that things are running down. But nothing can run down unless it has been wound up.

Now we hear from an eminent scientist, Dr. Edson Peck, a professor of physics at Northwestern University in Chicago, a member of the American Physical Society, the American Mathematical Society, and the Optical Society of America; a fellow of the American Association for the Advancement of Science and a member of Phi Beta Kappa, national honorary scholastic society. We quote him:

> We have good reason to believe that the universe is like a big clock engine that is slowly running down. Someone must have started it in motion. I believe that the starter was God.
>
> Support for this idea comes from an unchangeable principle known as the second law of thermodynamics.
>
> From *Scientists Who Believe*, C 1963
> David C. Cook Publishing Co.,
> Elgin, Il. 60120

However, if our world is the result of an evolutionary process it would be in a state of winding up, but it is not. It is winding down, which proves that it had to be wound up in the beginning.

2. *"God created the heaven and the earth,"* declares the

Bible (Gen. 1:1). There can be only two views of the origin of the world: one by creation, as stated in the Bible; the other by spontaneous generation in which something springs into existence from nothing, which has never been proved. Concerning the former, the highly regarded Wall Street Journal in a front page story, January 17, 1978, reported that the *Divine Creation* view is now presented in some college science courses. For years this explanation was largely untaught in college classes, but now is being given in courses at Michigan State, Iowa State and other schools. Some teach creation alongside the theory of evolution. It appears that the creation origin is a growing trend in education.

Christians understand by faith that the worlds were made by the word of God:

> Through faith we understand that the worlds were framed by the word of God, so that things which are seen were not made of things which do appear.
>
> — Hebrews 11:4

If this is wrong, suppose science prove to us that the earth originated in some other way. Their saying that the earth evolved does not help them. First, evolution is not a known fact of science — just a theory. Second, even if the earth had progressed from a tiny speck to its present state through billions of years of evolution, they still have the problem of explaining the origin of matter, unaided and untouched by a divine hand. They cannot!

The misunderstanding is partly due to the failure to distinguish between the permutation within a species and the evolution of a species. For instance, we can change the appearance and breed of dogs but they are still dogs. There is no known case of the transformation of species. There is no way scientists can start a new species and keep up the procreation.

3. *It has been said that the Biblical teaching on the age of the earth is not in agreement with science.* We reply: First, the Bible does not teach how old the earth is. Second, if it did, it would be impossible for the Bible to agree with scientists on this point for the simple reason that they are not agreed among themselves. Their estimates as to the age of the earth vary from about ten million years to about ten billion years. So it is preposterous for scientists to ask us if the Bible agrees with science on the age of the earth. We answer, what science?

(1) The Bible places the age of the earth back in the beginning. "In the beginning God created the heaven and the earth" (Gen. 1:1). Surely no scientist will ever uncover any fact that will cause him to contend that the earth is older than its "beginning." So the time stated in Genesis is safe.

(2) After the earth was created there was a chaotic period in which the earth was "without form, and void" (Gen. 1:2). This period existed after the creation "in the beginning" and before the first of the six creative days. This is very clear from a study of Gen. 1:1-5. The Bible does not tell us how long this disorganized state lasted. So no matter how old the scientists wish to place the earth, it will not contradict what the Bible says.

(3) Some have viewed the six days of creation mentioned in the Bible as six indefinite periods of time. This may or may not be true. The Hebrew word for "day" could bear such a meaning. We must admit that the all-powerful God could have chosen a long period of time to do a certain thing just as well as He could have chosen a day of twenty-four hours. For neither reflects upon the power of God, because He could have done all of it in a split-second instead of six days (whether days of twenty-four hours or longer) if He had wished. Either way, it pleased Him.

4. The Bible states, *"And the earth was without form, and void;* and darkness was upon the face of the deep" (Gen. 1:2). Science says that this is right, that the earth was once in a great turbulent condition preceding its present form as we know it today. Science says the earth was waste and void with neither vegetable nor animal life upon it. The Bible tells the same.

5. The Bible says, *"And the Spirit of God moved upon the face of the waters"* (Gen. 1:2). Geology calls this period the great ice age. Science says that ice and water covered the entire earth. Moses, who wrote Genesis, knew nothing of geology, but what he said is in perfect agreement with this science. The only possible explanation is that he was guided by the Lord.

6. The Bible account reads, *"And God said, Let there be light: and there was light . . ."* (Gen. 1:3-5). This was on the first day of creation, while the appearance of the sun is not mentioned until the fourth day of creation (Gen. 1:14-16). This has been a favorite target for disbelievers. They have asked, "How could light appear before the sun was created?" According to scientists, this was not difficult at all; for science has learned that there are other sources of light besides the sun, that the earth and other planets may be self-luminous. They have learned that this record in the Bible is possible. Moreover, it is strong evidence that Moses was inspired of God, for he surely would not have written from his own thinking that there was light before there was a sun. If he had been trying to perpetrate a religious fraud, he would not have stated what was considered at that time to be such an obvious error.

7. The Bible informs, *"And God said, Let there be a firmament in the midst of the waters, and let it divide the waters from the waters"* (Gen. 1:6). Science acknowledges two major bodies of water, one on earth and the other in the heavens. Moses says that the firmament was established to separate the

waters above from the waters below. Nature lifts the waters below to the waters above, and then allows such to return to the earth again. This is nature's way of watering the earth. It makes sense, and it is clearly set forth in the Bible.

8. *The Biblical order of creation is in full agreement with science:* (1) The world was created first (Gen. 1:1); (2) plant life was created next (Gen. 1:11-13); (3) the creation of fishes and fowls followed (Gen. 1:20-22); (4) animals were created last (Gen. 1:26,27). The sciences teach exactly the same succession. This perfect, scientific order set forth in the Bible before science ever figured it out is shocking to unbelieving scientists. Suppose they tell us how it got in the Bible back then.

9. Herbert Spencer, although he was an agnostic, announced in the nineteenth century *five categories which confirm the Biblical story of creation:* space, time, matter, force and motion. The Bible says, "In the beginning God created the heaven and the earth . . . and the Spirit of God moved upon the face of the waters" (Gen. 1:1,2). Let us notice the five distinct forms he suggested:

"In the beginning" .... Time.
"God created the heaven" .... Space.
"And the earth" .... Matter.
"And the Spirit of God" .... Force.
"Moved upon the face of the waters" .... Motion.

Before man learned this from a scientific viewpoint, the Bible had been telling man about it all along. True science is in agreement with the Bible. "Science falsely so called" is not in agreement even with itself.

CONCLUSION

It is evident that the religion of God, firmly rooted in common sense, has nothing to fear from the testing of ideas. Truth

The Biblical Account of Creation 23

never suffers from an honest, intelligent investigation. Error enslaves man, truth makes him free. "And ye shall know the truth, and the truth shall make you free" (John 8:32).

REVIEW EXERCISE

1. What are the only two possible views of the origin of the world?
   (1) .... (2) ....
2. Where does the Bible place the age of the earth? ....
   ....
3. How could there be light without the sun? ....
   ....
4. What is it that makes man free? ....
5. Give the five distinct, scientific areas mentioned in Gen. 1:1,2.
   (1) .... (2) .... (3) ....
   (4) .... (5) ....
6. Give the Biblical order of creation which in in agreement with science. ....
   ....
7. (T or F) The Bible speaks of a false science.
8. (T or F) The Genesis statement, "In the beginning" is absolutely scientific.
9. (T or F) Science's view that the earth was once in a chaotic, turbulent state is contrary to Biblical teaching.
10. (T or F) If evolution were true, there would be a winding up instead of a winding down of things.
11. Thought for discussion: Evolution is a theory instead of a known fact of science.
12. Thought for discussion: The true religion of God has nothing to fear from the testing of ideas.

III

That God Created Man Makes Sense

SINCE man is here, common sense tells us that he originated someway, somehow, and in some form. The question is, *How?* And the only rational answer is that he came from God, in God's likeness, as the Bible states:

> And God said, Let us make man in our image, after our likeness: and let them have dominion over the fish of the sea, and over the birds of the heavens, and over the cattle, and over all the earth, and over every creeping thing that creepeth upon the earth. And God created man in his own image, in the image of God created he him: male and female created he them.
> — Genesis 1:26,27

> And Jehovah God formed man of the dust of the ground, and breathed into his nostrils the breath of life; and man became a living soul.
> — Genesis 2:7

> What is man, that thou art mindful of him? Or the son of man, that thou visitest him? Thou madest him a little lower than the angels; thou crownedst him with glory and honor. And didst set him over the works of thy hands: Thou didst put all things in subjection under his feet.
> — Hebrews 2:6-8

The *mystery* of man is very comprehensible when we accept him as the created offspring of God (Acts 17:28,29). Nothing else is resolvable. For he could not have just happened.

However, science is still spending large sums of money probing, seeking an answer to what some call "the unexplained mystery of life." The majority of the scientists confess no real knowledge of life's origin, just some conflicting theories. Still they emphatically deny that it came through a miracle; but if they do not know, then how do they know life did not originate miraculously?

Life must have begun as an act of creation by the Creator or through spontaneous generation. One or the other. And there is nothing in science to lend even plausibility, let alone credibility, to the spontaneous generation theory. The great and governing laws of biology are that life can come from only life. The theory that natural forces originated life violates all the known facts of biology.

For dead matter (which the atheist cannot explain in the first place) to become alive, it would have to be quickened. If the various elements of the earth which are essential to life accidentally got together and were inexplicably quickened through natural means, we would have a phenomenon much harder to believe than the Biblical account of creation. To believe that the origin of all forms of life dates back billions of years to an unproved explosion of an unknown and unaccountable ball of life-giving particles requires a long stretch of imagination and a short spread of logic. It is much easier to believe the Biblical account.

We know that life is not now originating on earth, though scientists are trying to bring it about. They know what the necessary elements of life are and can bring them together, but they cannot breathe life into them. Life has not been created in a test tube, though there have been guided, scholarly efforts with the essentials.

Dr. Douglas Dean, of Pepperdine University, has stated in numerous lectures the following:

Contrary to popular belief, life has never been created in a test tube. Various news media may have reported that certain scientists have produced life, but it is also interesting to note that these scientists have emphatically denied that they created life. Some parts of living cells have been produced, but only after enzymes that came from living organisms were introduced. When these cell-derived enzymes were placed in the test tube, it was possible to duplicate certain functions or parts of living cells. But again we find life functions coming from pre-existing life. It has only been possible to duplicate life processes in a test tube when an enzyme which comes from some other living organism is introduced into that test tube. Thus, in reality, the scientist has not produced life. He has merely imitated cell functions using cell parts from some other source of life.

When the scientist seeks the origin of life, he can only determine that every living organism comes from living organisms.

Hence, the scientific principle that life can come only from life corroborates the Biblical exposition that a self-existent Life (God) created man.

MAN'S SPIRITUAL QUALITIES

Man has spiritual qualities that distinguish him from all other creatures. He is truly in a class by himself.

1. *Man has a spirit* (Eccl. 12:7). He is a twofold being — outward man and inward man, flesh and spirit: "Though our outward man perish, yet the inward man is renewed day by day" (II Cor. 4:16). As a dual being — outward and inward — each man has a heart. The heart of the outward man is the circulatory pump which keeps up the circulation of blood throughout the body; however, the heart or the seat of life of the inward man is that part of him with which he solves the issues of

life (Prov. 4:23) and distinguishes him as a creature made in the image of God.

2. *The spiritual attributes of man could not have come from dead matter.* A quality must have existed at least to some degree before it possibly could have evolved, even if evolution were true. Since dead matter has no spiritual qualities, then it would have been impossible for man's higher attributes to have evolved from lifeless matter. Spirit, emotions and conscience are attributes of God, and thus He is the only source from which man could have received them. Man has these spiritual attributes because they were breathed into him by his Creator (Gen. 2:7).

3. *It defies common sense to assume that man could have been endowed with spiritual qualities through an evolutionary process in which he made the long jump from the animal to man, entirely skipping over the missing link — the half-ape, half-man creature.* We still have both the animal and man in the world as they have always been known, but man has something the animal does not have — spiritual qualities. Animals are still animals with animal ways, and men are still men a little lower than angels. Animals still walk on four legs, but men walk upright and seek goals. Animals still rule in their kingdom by brute force, but man rules the world by the power of his mind (Gen. 1:26). Animals continue to find fulfillment and satisfaction in eating and whisking away the flies, but man's needs go deeper. "Man shall not live by bread alone" (Matt. 4:4).

The differences are so great that it would have been impossible for an animal to have turned into a man, spanning all this distance with no creature between the two. *And the evidence of the missing link is still unestablished.* Moreover, if an animal could have evolved into a half-animal, half-man creature, which evolved into a man, why isn't the process continuing today? Why aren't some of these half and half creatures here today? But they aren't. Neither can we find any of their remains.

Furthermore, another essential to its acceptability as science is the transmutation of species, which has not been proved. Dr. Thomas Hunt Morgan, of Columbia University, said:

> Within the period of human history we do not know of a single instance of the transformation of one species into another one.
> — *Evolution and Adaptation, p. 43*

GEOLOGICAL EVIDENCE FROM PAST AGES

1. *The Cambrian layer of the earth shows that life sprang suddenly into the world without progression, without evolution.* The creatures were complete and fully developed — no evolving from previous species. However, an examination of the rocks of the *pre-Cambrian* period — *Proterozoic Age* — fails to reveal that any life ever existed at that time. Thus it is evident that life in the *Cambrian Age* could not have evolved from the *Proterozoic Age*. This is most convincing.

2. *There is evidence from the fossils that the very lowest forms of life were fully developed with perfect organs that functioned.* To prove evolution, the remains would have to show an animal between a one cell animal and a perfect structure animal or organism, and such has never been found. Instead, the fossils show that the old creatures appeared in developed and fixed species, and that they have not evolved since. The life that existed millions of years ago, as seen in the strata, is the same as what you see today.

The crayfish in the Carboniferous Era and the whales of the Eocene Age are like the ones today.

The fossils reveal that in the *Silurian Age*, said to be nearly a hundred million years ago, there were the coral polyps and the algae working in the ocean then as now. Those little life forms have not changed in a hundred million years. In the light of this, the stock argument made by evolutionists that not enough time has passed to see the evolutionary process is evidently insupportable.

3. As seen, *nature's own records preserved in the rocks are in harmony with the Biblical account of creation* (Gen. 1). They tell us: (1) Life appeared suddenly. (2) Came fully developed. (3) Appeared in fixed units or species. (4) Plant life existed first; fishes, second; animals, third; and man, later — the very order stated in the first chapter of Genesis.

WHAT ABOUT THE APE-MEN?

1. *Have not the missing links between the apes and man been fully authenticated?* Are not their reconstructed forms in museums and their pictures in magazines and text books? No! What you see is only the manufactured creations of overworked imaginations of what their creators say must have existed. But the proof is lacking!

2. *A few facts about some of these reconstructed hypothetical creatures* are enlightening to the general public and embarrassing to their over-zealous creators:

(1) There is the *Nebraska Man*. He was represented as the oldest pre-historic man, a million years old. But the basis of this claim consisted of only one tooth discovered by Harold Cook in Nebraska. Only one tooth! Nevertheless, artists with a wild and preconceived imagination took that tooth and some plaster of Paris and made a creature they wanted in stature, posture, head, profile, complexion, hair and expression. Furthermore, they made him a wife out of nothing. (Not even God did that. He took man's rib to make Adam a wife.) And their pictures were run in the *Illustrated London News*, 1922. But time is revealing. The fossil that contained that tooth has

been found. It is the skeleton of an extinct pig. A pig's tooth! A contemptible hoax!

(2) The *Java Man* is the most famous of the supposed prehuman ancestors. It is assumed that he lived 750,000 years ago in Java. It was there that Dr. Eugene Dubois discovered him in 1891. But what was discovered? Now get this: only (1) a small piece of the top of a skull, (2) three molar teeth, and (3) a small portion of a left thigh bone. Furthermore, they were found scattered over a distance of at least fifty feet in an old river bed that contained much debris and many bones of extinct animals.

No wonder the scientists greatly differed on the discovery. Shortly afterwards, twenty-four of Europe's eminent scientists met and gave their conclusions: It was the opinion of seven that the bones belonged to an ape-man; ten thought they belonged to an ape; and the other seven thought they belonged to a man. No proof! Not even unanimity of opinion! Only assumption from a minority of overly biased wishers! Yet it is the basis of the renowned *Pithecanthropus Erectus* found in museums and books that assert the evolution of man. — W. A. Criswell, *Did Man Just Happen?*, pp. 83-85.

(3) Next, the *Neanderthal Man* has had an important place in text books and museums. The basis for this creature was dug up, 1857, in a small cave at the entrance of the Neanderthal gorge, Westphalia, Germany. Workers threw out some pieces of a skull bone. Scientists took the fragments and made a complete skull. Then they hastened to measure its internal capacity. The reason: the human skull is between 1400 and 1500 cubic centimeters while the ape's skull stops at 600 c.c. They wanted a skull between the two so they could tell the world they had found the missing link. The first measurement was 1033 c.c. But Professor Huxley himself estimated the capacity at 1230 c.c. Others went higher. Controversy has raged. There

have been twelve different opinions among most eminent scientists concerning this fragmented, humanly put-together skull. There are disputes about its age and its identity — whether the bones are human or animal or abnormalities. Another missing link is still missing. — G. C. Brewer, *Lecture on Evolution,* pp. 14,15.

(4) Also, the *Piltdown Man* has been introduced as evidence. He is supposed to have lived 300,000 to 500,000 years ago. A piece of skull bone was discovered, 1911, in a sand bed, Piltdown Common, Sussex, England. Anxious scientists subsequently found three other fragments: (1) another small piece of skull bone, (2) a part of a jaw-bone, and (3) one canine tooth. From this they made the *Piltdown* ape-man who got recognition in magazines, books and museums.

But in the *Reader's Digest,* October, 1956, there is an abridged article from the *Popular Science Monthly,* exposing this fraud under the caption, "The Great Piltdown Hoax." The humbug came to light. That piece of jaw bone was from an ape that had recently died. The teeth were filed down and along with the bones were artificially colored. Just another bogus link!

All of this makes you wonder how much real truth there is in some of the more recent claims for hypothetical ape-men, and what may come to light in another fifty years.

3. Now let us consider *some other thoughts, possibilities and facts* that are pertinent to this matter:

(1) It is obvious that circular reasoning has led evolutionists to hasty and unjustifiable conclusions. It goes like this: evolution must be true; therefore over a period of millions of years there must have been a succession of lower beings to the present man. Then the searchers seek specimens — even if it is no more than a tooth — to arbitrarily form a genealogical line.

The possibility of another explanation of the similarities in their line-up is not even considered.

(2) That there has been strong bias in forming humanity's imagined ancestry is most apparent. With only a few questionable twigs they have come up with an extensive genealogical tree. In fact, the more scarce and antiquated the remains of the fossils, the more sweeping are the conclusions. So their reconstructed ape-men recommend them more as artists than scientists.

(3) In keeping with this evident bias, the further the evolutionists go back the uglier they make the hypothetical ancestor of man and the bigger the club they give him to hold. They always put a club in his hand. All this is completely presumptive. There is no need for the ancients to be ugly. Neither is there a need for them to hold clubs. These are only evolutionary assumptions that fit their preconceived ideas.

(4) But here is something not presumptive — it is a fact that there can be considerable variableness within a species; and this counterargues the contention that a variant fossilized specimen is a sure link in the ancestral line of man. The questionable creature might be only a variant specimen within the species. Divergences of individuals within a single family of living apes today may be even greater than that observed in the fossils. So too much importance can be given to small differences between specimens, without which they would be considered a single species.

Of course, for a discoverer to claim he has found the missing link adds value to his find and prominence to his name.

(5) Furthermore, it is an undisputed fact that diet (soft or hard, raw or cooked) can affect teeth, causing longer and more pointed canines with greater projection. This has been confirmed in children that grew up with animals. — Arthur Cus-

tance, *Genesis and Early Man*, p. 200. Hence, to find a one-in-a-million skull with divergent teeth does not prove that it belonged to an intermediary ape-man.

(6) Neither is a fossilized heavier and broader lower jaw proof of the missing link. Today the Eskimo in the cold country has a heavier jaw than the person in the warm climate. The Eskimo's diet requires more chewing. There are dogs with different jaws but they are still dogs, and people separated by many ages in different climates with different diets are still people. And it is a known fact that whatever affects the jaw also affects an upward movement that influences the shaping of the skull.

(7) Likewise, the finding of skeletons of apes along with tools of the period does not prove that the creatures were intermediary ape-men with more intelligence than modern apes — thus the missing link. There is no proof the apish creatures manufactured the tools. They could have been manufactured and left by human hunters.

(8) Moreover, while it used to be considered that intelligence and cranial capacity were closely related, today it is highly questioned. Franz Weidenreich presented in one of his last writings the thought that there is no real correlation between cranial capacity and intelligence. — *The Human Brain in the Light of its Phylogenetic Development*, Sci. Monthly, Aug. 1948, pp. 103f.

Of course, it is agreed that the capacity can be so low (about 800 c.c.) as to make it impossible for one to be a normal human being.

So the smaller Australopithecine brain capacity might still be human. But in either case, it proves nothing because there are fossils with larger brain capacities contemporary with the smaller Australopithecine ones, which proves the smaller did not evolve into the larger for they were existing at the same time.

(9) Now here is evidence from the strata against the evolutionary descent of man. Mlle. Germaine Henri-Martin unearthed from a cave at Fontechevade in France a modern-type (note modern, not primitive) fossil from a level well below that where the Neanderthal Man is usually found. The fact that the bones came from below an undisturbed thick level of stalagmite guaranteed to anthropologists its genuine validity. — Loren Eiseley, *The Antiquity of Modern Man, Sci. American,* July 1948, pp. 16-19.

So here was proof that modern man could not have evolved from apish ancestors because the layers of rock had encased him first.

(10) Certainly there are living men today with the cranial appearance of the supposed apish creatures. Could not this have occurred in ages past, even in a more pronounced way?

The unusual growth of the pituitary gland produces caveman appearances like the enlarged chin, nose and brow. A well-known example is Maurice Tillet, a wrestler. He was once dressed up as a Neanderthal Man in a museum and passed as one of them. And when he stepped out from the still silence the shock of the spectators was overwhelming. Notwithstanding his unusual features, he was a university graduate. — Arthur Custance, *Genesis and Early Man,* pp. 217-219.

(11) Evolution cannot be experimentally demonstrated. The well-known geneticist and evolutionist, Richard B. Goldschmidt, has stated this. — Duane T. Gish, *How Life Began,* p. 168.

(12) After years of research, the evolutionary gaps are still there. With no traces of the intermediate links between the

major types of invertebrates or between invertebrates and vertebrates, the evidence is on the side of creation instead of evolution. If evolution is true, the museums should be filled with real (not man-made), easily recognizable intermediates. For instance, there should be a lot of part-fish, part-amphibian fossils, showing half-fins and half-feet. And there should be intermediates between the flying animal and its non-flying ancestor, which evolutionists need to dig up. But they haven't. Without the intermediates, evolution cannot be regarded as a scientific fact — just a theory. Creation makes more sense.

REVIEW EXERCISES

1. How is man a two-fold being? ....

2. Why is it the spiritual attributes of man could not have evolved from dead matter? ....

3. What did an eminent scholar say of the transmutation of species?

4. What do the layers of earth from the Cambrian and Proterozoic periods prove? ....

5. What four evidences from the records of the rocks are in harmony with the Biblical account of creation? (1) ....

    (2) .... (3) ....

    (4) ....

6. What was the basis for the reconstructed *Nebraska Man?* ....

7. What did the Reader's Digest reveal concerning the *Piltdown Man?*

8. What is the circular reasoning of the evolutionists? ....
   ....
9. What evidence was unearthed from a cave in France which proves that man did not evolve? ....
   ....
10. (T or F) Man was made a little higher than the angels.
11. (T or F) There are living men today with the cranial appearance of supposed ape-men.
12. Thought for discussion: Finding the smaller Australopithecine brain capacity does not prove the smaller type evolved into the larger type for they were existing at the same time.
13. Thought for discussion: If evolution is true, the museums should be filled with many real (not man-made), recognizable intermediates.
14. Thought for discussion: Creation makes more sense than evolution.

IV

Christ's Coming to Earth Makes Sense

THAT Christ existed before He was born of woman in Bethlehem is a clearly taught fact of Scripture. In describing Jesus as the Word, John said that He existed in the beginning (Jno. 1:1). Jesus Himself said: "Before Abraham was, I am" (Jno. 8:58); and, "O Father, glorify thou me with thine own self with the glory which I had with thee before the world was" (Jno. 17:5). Christ existed before the world was created. His being born of woman only marked the beginning of His life on earth.

CHRIST CAME TO EARTH

There is overwhelming evidence that Christ lived on earth:

1. *The name "Christian" has been worn for centuries.* Ancient history refers to this religious designation. It is a term that repeats the name of Christ, Christ-ian (Acts 11:26). It is unreasonable to assume that men and women back then would adopt the name of a man who never lived.

2. *The Lord's Day, the first day of the week,* would not have been set aside as a day of worship without a reason. Jews (those that first made up the church) had kept the Sabbath (seventh day) for centuries (Ex. 20:8). It stands to reason that some world-shaking event had to occur for man to change days for worship. It was the resurrection of Jesus. They celebrated His resurrection by having public worship on the day of the week He came forth — the Lord's Day (Rev. 1:10), the first day of the week (Matt. 28:1-6; Acts 20:7; I Cor. 16:2).

3. *For ages worshipers have taken the Lord's Supper in memory of Christ* (I Cor. 11:23-29). If He never lived and

died, how do we account for the beginning and continuance of this expressive memorial to Him?

4. *Time is dated B.C. (before Christ) and A.D.* — *Anno Domini (in the year of our Lord).* Anno Domini is an incontestible chronological fact. If He never came, what event shook society so hard that it started recording time on a different basis? And today an infidel cannot even date a letter without acknowledging that Jesus was born.

5. *Either Jesus came or else there is no sincerity in martrydom.* The writers of the New Testament said that Jesus lived and died. They should have known. They saw Him; they heard Him; they touched Him (I Jno. 1:1). There was no reason to misrepresent the facts, for their testimony cost them property and life. So either what they said is true or men had just as soon die for a lie as to die for the truth. Facing the lions in the arena, the pots of boiling oil, the fiery poles, and the torturous crosses, they refused to recant. Common sense tells us that they would not have chosen of their own free will to die in wholesale lots for Jesus, if they had not believed that He was real.

6. *In the field of secular history Josephus says:*

> Now there was about this time Jesus, a wise man, if it be lawful to call him a man; for he was a doer of wonderful works, a teacher of such men as receive the truth with pleasure. He drew over to him both many of the Jews and many of the Gentiles. He was [the] Christ. And when Pilate, at the suggestion of the principal men amongst us, had condemned him to the cross, those that loved him at the first did not forsake him; for he appeared to them alive again the third day; as the divine prophets had foretold these and ten thousand other wonderful things concerning him. And the tribe of Christians so named from him, are not extinct at this day.
>
> — Book 18, Chapter 3

Josephus lived about 37 A.D. to about 100 A.D. So this renowned historian who was not a Christian, thus not biased in favor of Christianity, had the opportunity to investigate the claims that were made relative to Christ by interviewing the very people who were eyewitnesses; and he says what the Gospels say about Jesus.

WAS HIS COMING RATIONAL?

Yes! It was in accord with a divine purpose and a wise plan of common sense.

After man had sinned in the Garden of Eden there was a need for a Saviour. Hence, immediately after the fall and in recognition of this necessity, God announced His intentions to send the Messiah, saying, ". . . it shall bruise thy head, and thou shalt bruise his heel" (Gen. 3:15).

Isaiah prophesied that the Saviour "was bruised for our iniquities . . . and the Lord hath laid on him the iniquity of us all" (Isa. 53:5,6). On Christ was laid the burden of man's iniquity and the divine plan to save man from it.

Fully aware of His mission, Jesus read from Isaiah's prophecy, 61:1,2, and applied it to himself:

> And there was delivered unto him the book of the prophet Esaias. And when he had opened the book, he found the place where it was written, The Spirit of the Lord is upon me, because he hath anointed me to preach the gospel to the poor; he hath sent me to heal the broken-hearted, to preach deliverance to the captives, and recovering of sight to the blind, to set at liberty them that are bruised, to preach the acceptable year of the Lord. And he closed the book, and he gave it again to the minister and sat down. And the eyes of all them that were in the synagogue were fastened on him.

> And he began to say unto them, This day is this Scripture fulfilled in your ears.
>
> — Luke 4:17-21

Thus Jesus acknowledged that He was the fulfillment of this prophecy which stated some of the purposes for which He came, the pivotal reason being "to set at liberty them that are bruised" by sin.

SOME REASONS CHRIST CAME

1. *To be an example.* Man's weak and frail nature called for a perfect pattern or example for him to follow. Jesus was it (I Pet. 2:21,22). His sinless steps were left on the sands of time for sinful man to find direction. Though this unique Man of Nazareth (the Son of man and the Son of God) was tempted in all points like as we are, He sinned not (Heb. 4:15).

In any production, construction or endeavor, a perfect blue print or pattern is needed. But there was no perfect example for living until the One "who went about doing good" (Acts 10:38) came to earth and walked and talked among men. "I find no fault in this man," was Pilate's verdict (Lk. 23:4).

2. *Jesus also came to give the complete and final will of God.* He is called "the Word." The Gospel of John is introduced with this thought: "In the beginning was the Word, and the Word was with God, and the Word was God" (Jno. 1:1). The term "Word" in the passage is capitalized. The translators knew that it is a title given to Christ. He is the Word, God's medium and power of communication to give a word-message to the world.

This Word role of Christ is further emphasized by Paul in his introduction of the Book of Hebrews: "God, who at sundry times and in divers manners, spake in times past unto the fathers by the prophets, hath in these last days spoken unto us by his son . . . the express image of his person" (Heb. 1:1-3). In these "last days" God spoke to the world through His Son who gave a better covenant enacted upon better promises (Heb. 8:6). The "last days" began on Pentecost — Peter's application of Joel's prophecy proves it (Acts 2:16,17). The Son's message is called *The New Testament* (Heb. 9:15). It was given by authority to save us (Jas. 1:21), and shall be opened by authority to judge us (Jno. 12:48).

Since His word is all-sufficient (II Tim. 3:16,17), then it is reasonable that no more would be given. He promised the apostles that they would be guided into "all truth" (Jno. 16:13). ALL! This left no new truth to be revealed.

3. *Unquestionably, the central and ultimate purpose of Christ's coming is to save man from the havoc wrought by sin and its necessary wages — eternal death* (Rom. 6:23). All other stated purposes are to achieve this one all-important design. He Himself said, "For the Son of man is come to seek and to save that which is lost" (Lk. 19:10). And when the self-righteous Pharisees condemned His disciples for eating with publicans and sinners, He responded, "They that are whole need not a physician; but they that are sick. I came not to call the righteous, but sinners to repentance" (Lk. 5:31,32). This prominent purpose of Christ's coming is beautifully accentuated in what man calls the "Golden Text" of the Bible, John 3:16, and the next verse which says, "For God sent not his Son into the world to condemn the world; but that the world through him might be saved" (Jno. 3:17). A mission of salvation! For man was spiritually lost!

Right here is a good place to correct a common error that reflects on the character of God. Men have been led to believe that God wants to destroy them, that God is anxious to pounce on man and cast him into an eternal damnation, and then sit back and gloat over it like a fiend feeds himself on another's miseries. No view of God is more perverted than this. It is the very opposite of God's wishes (I Tim. 2:3,4). But, of course, God never endorses the sinner's wrong doing. His justice, His righteousness, His respect for human volition, does not allow Him to connive at sin, nor to save a sinner against that sinner's will.

It is not humanly possible for us to accurately know the awfulness of sin and its just recompense. But it must be horrible, frightful, destructive, or God would not have sent His son to be born of a peasant woman, to live in the flesh, and finally to die on the cross to save man from it. For the Son to come and die needlessly would be an absurdity.

When we bear in mind man's lost and bankrupt state, his helplessness, his hopelessness, his inability to extricate himself, we can better appreciate the divine interposition. It was sin that reduced man to the state of an overburdened child of His Maker, just —

> A babe crying in the night,
> A babe crying for the light.

But man's condition was and is not one of despair, thanks be to divine grace.

Inasmuch as there was no life on earth — neither animal nor human — that qualified to atone for sin, it necessitated that Jesus come and ransom man. It was something He said He *ought* to do:

> Ought not Christ to have suffered these things, and to enter into his glory? . . . Then opened he their understanding, that they might understand the Scriptures, and said unto them, Thus it is written, and thus it behooved Christ to suffer, and to rise from the dead the third day: And that repentance and remission of sins

should be preached in his name among all nations, beginning at Jerusalem.

— Luke 24:26, 45-47

Ought means "to be necessary," and *behoove* means "to be necessary." It was absolutely essential!

4. It is frequently asked, *"Why wouldn't something besides the death of Christ resolve the problem of man's guilt?"* Here are some reasons:

(1) No animal could qualify to pay a huge debt for sin. First, the animals were not guilty — man was. Second, the beast devoid of a soul is not accountable to God. Third, the animal is not valuable enough to portray the enormity of sin. An animal would do for a type, but not for a redeemer. "For it is not possible that the blood of bulls and of goats should take away sins" (Heb. 10:4). Through the centuries animal sacrifices were but a faint acknowledgment of an unreconciled debt that defied complete forgiveness (Heb. 10:1). For if the guilty had been purged of sin, "then would they not have ceased to be offered" (Heb. 10:2)? In those animal sacrifices there was only "a remembrance again made of sins every year" (Heb. 10:3).

(2) An angel's dying would not have maintained the honor of God and satisfied the law of guilt, for we repeat — man was the guilty party.

(3) A special man was needed to offer his body as "one sacrifice for ever" (Heb. 10:10). And there was none to meet the requirements but Jesus.

(a) A man pure and holy, with all his powers unimpaired by sin as Adam was before the fall, was required. Only Jesus qualified (I Pet. 1:18-20).

(b) There was a need for a man, representative of the race

as Adam was in its fall. "For as in Adam all die, even so in Christ shall all be made alive" (I Cor. 15:22).

(c) Inasmuch as Adam's rebellion was a voluntary act while in the full use of all his undebased faculties, then a perfect equivalent was required in which a redeemer with unimpeded aptitudes would present himself. So it was with Christ who declared, "I lay down my life . . . No man taketh it from me, but I lay it down of myself" (Jno. 10:17,18).

(d) A redeemer must be free of transgression, or else his death would be for himself and there would be no life left to give for others. Besides Jesus, there was none devoid of sin (Rom. 3:23).

(e) A redeemer and mediator must be equally connected with both parties. Only Jesus was prepared for this role (I Tim. 2:5,6). He was the Son of man and the Son of God: the "Son of man" by reason of the fact that His mother was a human — not a deity — with the faculties of any other woman; and the "Son of God" in that He was begotten by the Holy Spirit (not by a man), thus born of a virgin (Matt. 1:20-23). To contend that Mary was a deity attacks God's plan of redemption. For Jesus to have been begotten by a man or to have been born of a deity would have voided the necessary character of an equidistant mediator.

(f) Had Jesus been all *divine*, His death would not have appeased the broken law for man. Had He been all *human*, He would not have satisfied the requirement for perfection, nor would He have been raised from the dead for lack of power — a necessary declaration of His Sonship and an essential hope for the redeemed: "Declared to be the Son of God with power . . . by the resurrection from the dead" (Rom. 1:4).

Hence, Christ's coming to earth with His two natures and

His filling the essential roles of living, teaching, dying and coming forth from the dead makes sense!

REVIEW EXERCISE

1. Jesus said that He existed "before the ....
   .... Scripture: ....
2. What unusual event caused the day of worship to be changed from the seventh day to the first day? ....
3. What does *Anno Domini* prove? ....
4. What did Josephus say of Christ? ....
   ....
5. What prophecy did Jesus apply to Himself concerning His coming to earth? ....
6. Give three reasons for Christ's coming to earth. (1) ....
   .... (2).................. (3)..................
7. Give three reasons why an animal could not qualify to redeem man. (1) .... (2) ....
   (3) ....
8. Give four reasons why that only Christ could qualify as man's redeemer. (1)...
   (2) ....
   (3) ....
   (4) ....
9. Explain why man could not have been redeemed by one who was either all *divine* or all *human*. ....
   ....

10. (T or F) Jesus never had a "Word" role on earth.
11. (T or F) Christ said that He "ought" to die and rise from the dead.
12. Thought question: Do many people think that God is anxious to to pounce on man and cast him into damnation?

V

Common Sense Demands the Bible

IT makes sense that God gave man the Bible. If there is a God who created the earth, it is reasonable that He would create man for its rulership, which necessitated that He give him appropriate qualities. Thus man was endowed with a mind that gives him great reasoning power and a vision to plan toward distant goals. He has a conscience affected by the past, a consciousness that weighs upon the present, and an immortal longing that beckons to the future.

Now I challenge your logic. Is it not a matter of common sense that the Creator would reveal Himself to this type of man in a concrete and definite way as the Bible does?

MAN'S NEED REQUIRES THE BIBLE

1. *If God has not revealed Himself as the Bible indicates,* then we cannot know His mind toward us, or what we are, or why we are here, or from whence we came, or where we are going. Without a revelation from God, our existence is a fathomless riddle, life a dark mystery, and death a frightful leap into dreadful darkness. So it is reasonable that whatever is necessary for man, God would provide — thus the Bible.

2. While *nature* testifies to God's existence and power (Psa. 19:1), it *does not relate God's will to us.* So in addition to the testimony of nature, God has given His Holy Word to fill a purpose.

3. *Man needs a revelation on tne concrete certainties of religion.* Hence, the design of God's revealed Word is to pro-

duce: (1) *knowledge* ("Ye do err, not knowing the Scriptures," Matt. 22:29); (2) *faith* (which comes by "hearing the word of God," Rom. 10:17); and (3) all that accompanies in human *duty* ("Fear God, and keep his commandments," Eccl. 12:13), and in human *hope* ("Looking for that blessed hope," Tit. 2:13), and in human *destiny* ("man goeth to his long home," Eccl. 12:5).

When His Word is known and believed, it brings home to man's heart the glorious essentials that help him to deal with life's realities by exerting an appreciative and controlling influence over his affection, will and conduct.

4. *The Bible is the Success Book which turns man's defeats into victories.* His forlorn failures with all their terrors and agonies are everywhere. But the Word of God has never reaped a failure.

An infidel who was a soap manufacturer once said to a preacher, "That Bible you preach is a failure. There are lots of unclean people in the world." Just at that time a child with a dirty face walked in front of them. The preacher pointed to the child and said, "That soap of yours is a failure." "Oh, no," replied the soap man, "it's the fault of the people for not using it." Therein is the explanation of man's spiritual dirt; but, thanks be to the grace of God, there is available to him a cleansing power more effective than any soap. "Now ye are clean through the word which I have spoken unto you" (Jno. 15:3).

EVIDENCES OF INSPIRATION

There are statements in and facts concerning the Bible that we are unable to account for except in the light of inspiration. Consider:

1. *The fulfillment of prophecies:*

(1) That Christ would be born of a virgin (Isa. 7:13,14). Fulfilled (Lk. 1:26-35).

(2) That Christ would be born in Bethlehem (Mic. 5:2). Fulfilled (Matt. 2:1-11).

(3) The distinct entry of Jesus into Jerusalem (Zech. 9:9,10). Fulfilled (Matt. 21:1-9).

(4) The betrayal of Christ by a familiar friend (Psa. 41:9). Fulfilled (Mk. 14:43-49).

(5) That the price of betrayal would be thirty pieces of silver (Zech. 11:12,13). Fulfilled (Matt. 27:3-10).

(6) That they would cast lots for His clothes (Psa. 22:18). Fulfilled (Jno. 19:23,24).

There are many others. They had to be inspired, for uninspired men could not have known.

2. *The authoritative nature of the Bible attests to its inspiration.* This is a characteristic not found in human books. The Bible claims to be from God, the source of all authority. "Thus saith the Lord" is repeated nearly two thousand times. In contrast with human writers, the Bible is definite and certain. It is no book of conjectures. It even speaks of the future as positively as if it had already occurred.

3. *Its complete impartiality* is uncharacteristic of human books. The same Bible that portrays Abraham as the father of the faithful does not overlook his sin. And David, a man after God's own heart, is also pictured as the perpetrator of the vilest of evils. The Bible gives the whole truth, the good and the bad, concerning man. "God is no respecter of persons" (Acts 10:34).

4. *The declaration that the world had a beginning* indicates divine authorship (Gen. 1:1). After years of research, more

scientists finally came to the conclusion of what the Bible had been saying all along in its very first statement.

5. *Its assertion that the creation of matter preceded order* denotes inspiration. Before science learned this, the Bible was saying, "earth was without form and void" (Gen. 1:2).

6. *The statement that light existed before the sun* (Gen. 1:3) could not have come from man's knowledge. Laplace authored the nebular hypothesis that "the condensation of gaseous matter was accompanied by intense heat — emitting light." But before Laplace dreamed of it, Moses stated it.

7. *The true order of creation* (Gen. 1,2) baffles unbelieving scientists. They are still trying to figure out how Moses knew. See p. 22.

8. *Statements on the rotundity of the earth* bespeaks the Bible's divinity. At a time when man thought the earth was flat, the Bible declared that it is circular (Isa. 40:42). In speaking of His second coming, Jesus affirmed that He would come in the day and in the night (Lk. 17:31,34). Back when this was written no human being knew the earth was round and that it is day on one part while it is night on the other part.

9. *The teaching on the sudden and complete destruction of the earth* proclaims a super-human knowledge: "The heavens shall pass away with a great noise, and the elements shall melt with fervent heat" (II Pet. 3:10). For centuries the enemies of the Bible derided the thought. But now, since science has learned something of the splitting of the atoms, it is conceded as a scientific possibility. No man would have written at that time what was considered to be a certain impossibility. Only God could have known to write it.

10. *The harmony of the Bible* attests to its divinity. Though it was written by about forty different writers over a period of

about sixteen centuries, a single purpose and unity run throughout the whole book. That purpose is to bring man nearer to God and to God's blessings, by teaching him how to live and how to die — to live in faith and to die in hope. That some forty writers, mostly unknown to each other, living in different ages and circumstances, laboring under divergent customs and governments, should have written a sublime book that pursued one principal object is more than an accidental occurrence! more than a human production!

THE INSPIRED BIBLE

1. *The fallibility of man* ("For all have sinned," Rom. 3:23) *requires an infallible guide* ("The law of the Lord is perfect," Psa. 19:7). Man is subject to flesh's errors and time's decay. Our lives are full of mistakes that plague us. How tottering and feeble we are. So mankind requires a standard that is reliable and lasting. Only a Bible from God could fill that requisite. A strictly human Bible would be as erroneous as man, which would amount to one imperfect person's telling another imperfect person what to do. The mistakes of the authors would become the mistakes of the readers. This makes no sense at all. But if it came from God, we have the *perfect* instructing the *imperfect*. Now that makes sense.

So, amid all the blunders of man and the ruins of his dream castles, it is the Bible alone that stands like a tower, higher than the heavens, brighter than the sun and as immutable as the rock of ages (Matt. 24:35), to which man may turn for a complete and perfect guide (Psa. 119:105). For it to serve its purpose it had to be perfect; and perfection demanded the authorship of the God who cannot lie (Tit. 1:2). This gives us confidence in its utterances.

2. *The inspiration of the Bible is essential to its authority.* An uninspired Bible would be strictly suggestive — no binding

commands — with every thesis and overtone being only advisory. And its reaches for immortality would stretch no farther than the limits of a man's vision.

Common sense requires authoritative standards in various fields: time, weights and measures and likewise religion.

We would not think of going to the writings of Aristotle to find an answer to the question, "What must I do to be saved?" (Acts 16:30). Or to Horace to ascertain the answer to the issue, "For what shall it profit a man, if he shall gain the whole world, and lose his own soul?" (Mk. 8:36). Or to Shakespeare to get a solution to the age-old problem that presses every generation, "If a man die, shall he live again?" (Job 14:14).

Human writings will not suffice for authority. We demand the divine. This is why the Bible continues to be such a popular book that remains through the ages — its authoritative nature. While the volumes of the moralists and philosophers make their appearance with all the noise and glamour of a military band, there is a good chance that they will later limp off the stage of action like consumptive freaks. But the Bible continues to march with the changing times and is ever cherished as the one great authoritative book of the past, the present and the future! The reason — it is from God!

3. *The Bible is unique in that it is perfectly divine* (God the inspirer) *and necessarily human* (man the agent). While man is the medium through which the Bible came, he is neither its source nor its authority. God merely used humans as the instrumentality to convey His Word to the world (II Pet. 1:21). Human beings wrote every word of the Bible, but the Holy Spirit directed them.

(1) The Holy Spirit moved man to write God's prophecy (II Pet. 1:21).

(2) The Holy Spirit guided the apostles into *all* truth (Jno. 16:13).

(3) Peter asserted that those who preached the gospel did so through "the Holy Ghost sent down from heaven" (I Pet. 1:12).

(4) Paul affirmed that he preached the certified gospel: "not after man. For I neither received it of man, neither was I taught it, but by the revelation of Jesus Christ" (Gal. 1:11,12).

(5) John declared that the Revelation was given him by the Lord, that it was a communication of the Spirit (Rev. 1:1; 2:7).

(6) In declaring the utility, inspiration and completeness of all Scripture, Paul said that it was "given by inspiration of God" (II Tim. 3:16,17).

4. *The Bible is verbally inspired in the original languages.* The plenary inspiration of the Scriptures is essential to any inspiration at all. If the writers were not inspired word for word, what assurance do you have that erring humans, unaided by divine power, chose the correct words to convey the divine message? I ask, does it make sense that God would inspire the writers in perfect thoughts and then leave the revelation of those thoughts to the imperfect wording of man? In that case, the world would have the inspired thought of God and the uninspired word of man. The latter could have destroyed the former.

(1) In sending out the disciples, Jesus said, "Take ye no thought how or what thing ye shall answer, or what ye shall say: For the Holy Ghost shall teach you in the same hour what ye ought to say" (Lk. 12:11,12). The *how* a thing is said involves the wording of it. The Holy Spirit took care of the *how,* inspiring them in the selection of the words used.

(2) Paul claimed that the Holy Spirit taught them the things

to speak, "not in the words which man's wisdom teacheth, but which the Holy Ghost teacheth" (I Cor. 2:13).

(3) Irrefutable evidence for verbal inspiration is the apostles' speaking in unknown tongues (foreign languages) they did not know. Indeed, if they had been inspired only in thought, how did they speak in foreign words they did not understand? There is no way they could have spoken an unknown language without verbal inspiration — "as the Spirit gave them utterance" (Acts 2:4).

(4) It is called "the word of the Lord" (II Thess. 3:1) — not the thought of the Lord and the word of man.

(5) If God would open the mouth of a dumb donkey to communicate a true message, Num. 22:28 (surely no one would argue that the thought was inspired, while the wording was left up to the donkey), then why should we think that God would not use a man to do the same?

(6) But some ask: "If the Bible is verbally inspired, why does each book show the writer's individual vocabulary and background? Why wouldn't every book have the same style?" Because the Infinite wanted to reveal Himself to the finite in the most effective manner. To do this, He employed the languages, vocabularaies, customs and backgrounds of the finite — human beings. For Him to have developed and used an infinite language to express Himself to finite people would have been unworkable and absurd.

Inspiration did not disregard individual education, vocabulary, training and environment. God used these men as they were in giving His Written Word, just like He used the natural voices of the men in communicating the oral Word. There is no reason to believe He changed the voices of the speakers from high to low or vice versa. Neither did He change the authors' vocabularies and backgrounds. He preferred to use them as He found them, guarding over their usage of the right word.

Indeed, only God could make a book both human and divine at the same time!

> Hast thou ever heard
> Of such a Book? the Author — God himself,
> The subject — God and man, salvation, life,
> And death — eternal life, eternal death —
> Dear words! whose meaning has no end, no bounds!
> Most wondrous Book! bright candle of the Lord!
> Star of eternity! the only star
> By which the bark of man could navigate
> The sea of life, and gain the coast of bliss
> Securely.

REVIEW EXERCISE

1. "Ye do err, not knowing the ...."

2. How does faith come? ....

3. What did Jesus say that proves He knew the earth is round?
   ....

4. What did Peter say about the complete destruction of the earth that was once thought to be unscientific?...........................
   ....

5. Why does man demand an inspired authoritative Bible? ....
   ....

6. How is the Bible perfectly divine and necessarily human? ....
   ....

7. Why would the Bible have to be verbally inspired to be inspired at all? ....

8. (T or F) All we need to tell us of God's will is nature.
9. (T or F) The fulfillment of prophecies is one of the proofs the Bible is inspired.
10. (T or F) A characteristic of the Bible not found in other books is its authoritative nature.
11. (T or F) The Bible does not say that it is inspired.
12. Thought question: How would man's fallibility be compounded if the Bible were imperfect?

VI

Common Sense Requires Right Division of Bible

THE Author of the Bible commanded it: "Study [give diligence, A.S.V.] to show thyself approved unto God, a workman that needeth not to be ashamed, rightly dividing the word of truth" (II Tim. 2:15).

THIS IS SENSIBLE

1. *Now we appeal to reason and common sense* to back up the absolute necessity and practicality of "rightly dividing the word of truth." This principle is understood the world over in the interpretation of all human writings. Surely the saneness of such is just as great in handling the Word of God.

2. *To mishandle it is dangerous.* The Bible describes itself as "quick [living], and powerful, and sharper than any two-edged sword" (Heb. 4:12). A two-edged sword is dangerous if a person knows nothing about handling it. Thus to avoid the dangers inherent in the use of this two-edged sword — the Bible — each person should give diligence to rightly divide it.

Dr. William Lyons has said that there should be written across the cover of every Bible these words:

> Highly explosive; handle with care.

3. Common sense tells us that God's giving the Scriptures to man places on him *the unavoidable responsibility* of coming to grips with the problem of interpreting them correctly. And logic tells us that man can; for if he cannot, they are of no value whatever to him.

4. *When one person writes another,* he does it on the full assumption that his message can be interpreted and understood. To discredit God by supposing He has less intelligence than a man is unthinkable. And it does dishonor to God for us to presume that He has given a Book that cannot be understood.

He expects it to be understood:

(1) When Philip was sent to preach to the Ethiopian treasurer, whom he found reading the Bible, his first words were: "Understandest thou what thou readest" (Acts 8:30)? He didn't, but he could; and since he could, Philip began at the same Scripture and preached unto him.

(2) In the necessary steps to conversion, Jesus included understanding which is preceded by teaching (Matt. 13:15).

(3) While Peter said that some things are hard to understand, he did not say that it is impossible to comprehend them; he rather said that it is the unlearned who wrest or twist these Scriptures, not the learned: "As also in all his epistles, speaking in them of these things; in which are some things hard to be understood, which they that are unlearned and unstable wrest, as they do also the other Scriptures, unto their own destruction (II Pet. 3:16).

5. Inasmuch as God saw fit to give the Scriptures in human language, spoken by men to men, (see Chapter V), then it is rational to proceed on the basis that each book of the Bible, when interpreted by *the common rules and usages of the language of that day,* is intelligible and ascertainable like any other book. Deeper! More profound! Inexhaustible! The Book from which no scholar ever graduates! But clothed in the same comprehensible wordage as other books.

6. *To contend that a miraculous interposition* is needed to

teach a person the art of interpreting the Scriptures raises the question as to why they were given in the first place. For if a miracle is needed to interpret them, then this would make the Bible a revelation that has to be revealed, which would be no revelation at all. Truly there is no greater abuse of revelation than to assume that it does not reveal.

7. If the human family had spoken and had continued to speak *only one language* and had it remained unchanged, then there never would have been a need for translations; and if the meaning of words and the customs of people had remained the same down to this present time, the matter of interpretation would be much simpler. However, it is still within our grasp.

8. Though we understand exactly what a passage says, we cannot fully perceive through our finite reasoning the "how" of the workings of the Infinite. But when we view His glorious works *through the eye of faith,* we see what corporeal senses never perceive. In speaking of this kind of perception, Paul said, "Through faith we understand that the worlds were framed by the word of God, so that things which are seen were not made of things which do appear" (Heb. 11:3). It is easy to understand the words and phrases in this verse; but to *really* comprehend it faith is needed. So many times it is not a question of whether we understand a verse, but rather, do we believe it?

RELIGIOUS DISPENSATIONS OF THE BIBLE

Suppose a policeman who has been searching old city ordinances finds one passed in 1912 that prohibits driving a car on California Street in this Texas town, and now he dashes out to enforce it. Later it is explained to him that the law was proper in its time (even helpful) for it prevented the horses on the street from being scared, but that now it is no longer binding by virtue of the fact that it has been annulled and is a repealed law. Now shall he say, "A law is a law and it doesn't make any difference to me whether it has been invalidated or not?" No, he has more sense than that.

We appeal to the same common sense in the study of the Bible. We ask, under which dispensation was the commandment given? Is it binding on us today?

It is indispensable, therefore, that we learn there are three religious ages or dispensations spoken of in the Bible, each with several distinctions:

1. *Patriarchal.* Patriarch means father. He was the head of the family or tribe. Under this system, he directed the family both politically and religiously. He was ruler, priest and prophet. They had no written system of religion; instead, God spoke to the patriarch orally and he communicated the message to the family. Consequently, what was a law to one patriarch may not necessarily have been a law to other patriarchs. As an example, Noah was commanded to build an ark, but the other patriarchs were not given such a command. This system lasted from Adam to the giving of the Jewish law at Mt. Sinai; and apparently continued among the Gentiles until the death of Christ. The forms of idolatry that later developed among the Gentile nations were only the corruptions of this religion.

2. *Jewish dispensation.*

(1) One of the distinctions of this religious government is that it was Jewish, given to the Jews, the descendants of Abraham. God promised Abraham, "In thy seed shall all the families of the earth be blessed" (Gen. 12;3; 22:18). In order then to keep this promise, it was necessary to separate Abraham's descendants from all other nations until the Messiah, the promised seed or descendant, should come; or, as Paul worded

it, "until the seed should come to whom the promise was made" (Gal. 3:19). This characteristic exclusiveness of the Jewish law is spoken of as "the middle wall of partition between" the Jews and others (Eph. 2:14).

(2) Instead of the family system, it was enlarged into a national system, in keeping with the promise made to Abraham (Gen. 12:2).

(3) As another peculiarity, for the first time man was given a written religion. At the foot of Mt. Sinai, God gave them the Ten Commandments written upon two tables of stone (Ex. 19, 20). This was the beginning of "book" religion. Incidentally, "book" religion is something God has favored (Jno. 20:30,31).

(4) The Jewish or Mosaic law was faulty (Heb. 8:7). One evident weakness was no complete forgiveness of sins — they just lived and died in the promise of remission. "Impossible that the blood of bulls and goats should take away sins"; so the continuous offering of animal sacrifices only moved forward the sins year by year (Heb. 10:1-4). Nothing but the blood of Christ could blot out sin (Heb. 10:11,12; 9:11-14).

(5) Another object of the Jewish law was to be a schoolmaster or tutor to train and educate man to receive Christ (Gal. 3:24). From the training under the first covenant, man was prepared for the second.

(6) The Jewish covenant is called "the old testament . . . done away in Christ" (II Cor. 3:14), while the covenant given by Christ is called "the new testament" (Heb. 9:15). Though "the old testament" is the second religion of the Bible (the first being the Patriarchal), it is called the "first" because it was the first written covenant; and though the "new" is the third, it is called the "second" because it is the second written covenant. Jesus abolished the "first" and gave the "second"

— "he taketh away the first, that he may establish the second" (Heb. 10:9).

(7) Since "the old testament" was to last only until Christ came (Gal. 3:19), then when He came He nailed it to the cross (Col. 2:14) — that is, when He died, it died. It is now an abrogated law.

3. Christian dispensation.

(1) It is called "Christian" because it was given by Christ (Heb. 10:9; 8:6,7). In these last days God has spoken to the world through His Son (Heb. 1:1,2).

(2) It is the last religious age or dispensation. Its beginning (on Pentecost following the resurrection of Jesus) was the beginning of the last days (Acts 2;16,17). Man lived under the days of the Patriarchal age; and under the days of the Jewish age; and now he lives under the Christian dispensation — "the last days" — and when these days are over, there will be no more days, just eternity. Consequently, the teachings under this religion will last until the end of time. Jesus declared, "Heaven and earth shall pass away, but my words shall not pass away" (Matt. 24:35).

(3) This dispensation assures the complete forgiveness of sins: for the alien (Acts 2:38; 22:16), and for the erring Christian (Acts 8:22; I Jno. 1:7-9).

(4) The religion of Christ is for all peoples and all nations (Matt. 28:19,20; Gal. 3:28).

(5) It could not become operational, however, until after the death of Christ. To enforce this truth, Paul used a simple illustration from everyday life: "For where a testament is, there must also of necessity be the death of the testator. For a testament is of force after men are dead: otherwise it is of no strength at all while the testator liveth" (Heb. 9:16,17). The

whole world says this makes sense. As long as the maker of the will is alive, he can do as he wishes with what is his; but after the will is sealed by his death, it must be carried out according to its provisions. Paul insists that the same logic applies to Christ's testament. When Christ was alive in the flesh on earth, He could say, as He did to the thief on the cross, "This day shalt thou be with me in paradise" (Lk. 23:43). But now He is not in the flesh. Now, to obtain salvation, the provisions of His will must be followed.

It makes for understanding to keep in mind that the thief and multitudes of others lived and died under the Patriarchal and Jewish laws which did not require baptism in the name of the Father, Son and Holy Spirit, for the remission of sins. Abraham, Isaac, Jacob, David and even the thief were not commanded many things we are commanded and vice versa. The reason — the laws are different.

(6) The general principles of religion have ever been the same in all three religious ages, though the rites, ceremonies and procedures have changed. As examples:

There was a time when God commanded people to offer animal sacrifices (Lev. 3-5), but today each is commanded to present his body as a living sacrifice (Rom. 12:1).

Formerly, man kept the Sabbath (seventh day), which is the only one of the Ten Commandments not carried over in teaching form to the New Testament. However, today under the New, we meet for worship on the first day of the week (Acts 20:7; I Cor. 16:2).

Circumcision was once commanded (Ex. 17:10), but under the Christian religion the real *Jew* or child of God is one who is such inwardly — whose mark of such is not on the flesh but on the heart (Rom. 2:28,29).

(7) Now here is some saneness on consistency: "For I testify again to every man that is circumcised, that he is a debtor to do the whole law" (Gal. 5:3). Paul is saying that the person who goes back to the Old Testament for his authority for circumcision or any other religious rite or practice not taught in the New is faced with a consistency problem. Uniformity demands that he accept all — animal sacrifices, sprinkling of blood, etc., as well as circumcision — not just pick out what he wants. If you are going to keep a portion of the Old Testament, logic says that you are a debtor to do all of it. This was Paul's argument. And it makes sense.

While much of the teachings in the Old are included in the New, it definitely remains that unless a thing *is* taught in the New it is not binding on us today.

NECESSARY ATTITUDES IN BIBLE STUDY

What some think are discrepancies in the Bible are actually deficiencies in the mind and heart of the reader. God cannot lie (Tit. 1:1,2). But the mind of man can err, even when sincere, and is sure to blunder when it is not. So it is fitting that we consider at least four attitudes that should prevail as we endeavor to learn and rightly divide the Bible:

1. *A consciousness of the absolute necessity of a correct understanding of God's word.* Unacquaintance of the Word has ever been characteristic of many people. "But Israel doth not know, my people doth not consider" (Isa. 1:3). In axiomatic form, Hosea stated, "My people are destroyed for lack of knowledge" (Hos. 4:6).

One of man's worst enemies is unacquaintance with facts. Ignorance of the laws of health blindly leads people to early graves. Unenlightenment of the Bible leads people to do the exact opposite of what God teaches, and all the more pitiful, many think they are doing God a service (Jno. 16:2,3).

2. *Faith*. We should approach Bible study with complete faith in it, believing — no matter who is right or wrong — the Bible is right. This will cause us to seek an interpretation that sees the unity of Scriptures rather than man-made contradictions that come from pitting one Scripture against another.

For instance, the Bible says we are justified by *faith* (Rom. 5:1). It also states that we are justified by *works*, not by faith only (Jas. 2:24). Rather than set the two verses in opposition to each other, is it not more sensible to say that faith justifies when it works? That was when faith saved Noah (Heb. 11:7); and that was when the walls of Jericho fell (Heb. 11:30). Furthermore, it is evident that when Paul speaks of salvation by faith, he means an obedient faith. In Rom. 1:5, he says, "obedience to the faith"; and in 16:26, "the obedience of faith." So the contradictions, as in this case, are not in the Scriptures but in man's interpretations.

3. *Freedom from prejudice.* Prejudgment obstructs learning. Jesus said, "For this people's heart is waxed gross, and their ears are dull of hearing, and their eyes they have closed" (Matt. 13:15). Prejudice has stopped many an ear and closed many an eye. The results have been tragic.

The spectacles of bias color the text. As an example, put on brown glasses and everything seems brown; blue ones and everything appears blue; green ones and everything is shaded green. What is seen is determined by the eyes that do the looking and the glasses through which they look. This is why some people see in the Bible what others do not. The difference is not in the object but in the eyes. So common sense tells us that if we would see God's word in its true tint, we must remove the biased spectacles of church creeds and other preconceptions.

4. *A desire to obey.* It is useless to learn truth unless we intend to apply it to ourselves. Jesus said, "If any man will

do his will, he shall know of the doctrine, whether it be of God, or whether I speak of myself" (Jno. 7:17). He who studies the Bible with an inclination to obey is on the road to knowledge.

REVIEW EXERCISE

1. What is sharper than any two-edged sword? ....
2. Why would the Bible· be of no value to man if it could not be interpreted correctly? ....
   ....
3. What did Philip say to the Ethiopian treasurer which shows he expected the Bible to be understood? ....
   ....
4. What are the three religious ages or dispensations? (1) ....
   .... (2) .... (3) ....
5. Give four distinctions of the Jewish dispensation. (1) ....
   .... (2) ....
   (3) .... (4) ....
6. The Jewish covenant is called "the old testament ... .
   .... in Christ."
7. What had to occur before the New Testament could go into effect? ....
8. What is the consistency of which Paul speaks in Gal. 5:3? ....
   ....
9. How long was the Old Testament to last? ....
10. (T or F) Paul commanded that the word of truth be rightly divided.
11. Thought for discussion: If a miraculous interposition is needed to

understand the Bible, then it would be a revelation that has to be revealed.
12. Thought for discussion: How can a failure to rightly divide the Bible bring on many other errors?

VII
The Church Makes Sense

WHEN we understand the meaning of the church, its structure, duties, functions and hope, we shall perceive that it was a profound, sensible act on the part of the Lord to establish it.

IT WAS RATIONAL TO ESTABLISH JUST ONE CHURCH

In a religiously divided home a father customarily took a little boy and went to one church, while the mother took the little girl and attended another. This incongruousness produced an unpleasantness which prodded the little girl to outthink her parents and a world of other adults. One day she asked, "Mother, if God does all things well, why didn't He build just one church so we could all go to church together?"

Well, the truth of the matter is, He did. And it makes sense.

1. *Jesus promised to build one church:* "Upon this rock I will build my church" (Matt. 16:18). He said *C-H-U-R-C-H*. This is singular, means *one*.

2. When the promise to build it was fulfilled on Pentecost, "The Lord *added to the church* daily such as should be saved" (Acts 2:47). The Lord adds people to only one church — not to denominations. Men founded them, and to them men must do the adding.

3. Jesus "purchased with his own blood" *the church* of God (Acts 20:28). *One!*

4. *The Bible repeatedly says there is one body:* "For as we have many members in one body . . ." (Rom. 12:4,5). See

I Cor. 12:20 and Eph. 2:16. In the passage in which Paul speaks of *one* God, *one* Lord, *one* Spirit, he also speaks of *one* faith, *one* baptism and *one* body (Eph. 4:4-6). There are no more divinely given faiths, baptisms and bodies than there are Gods, Christs and Spirits. Just one! It is contrary to reasonableness for people to be divided into sects. If one man should "join" every church in town and preach one doctrine one time and the opposite the next time, would you go hear him? "Of course not," you say. "Because he has no convictions. He contradicts himself. He is a hypocrite." But if it is wrong for one man to do this, then would it not be wrong for one God to do it, to call one man to deny what He calls another to affirm? Ordinary sense tells us that God would not oppose God.

5. *Unity is taught in the figure of the sheepfold:* "And they shall hear my voice; and there shall be one fold, and one shepherd" (Jno. 10:16). The Bible presents one Shepherd and one fold, not many folds with different kinds of sheep. All the sheep are in one fold. The reason — they heard the voice of the one Shepherd. Many different folds today is evidence that people have heard the voices of men instead of Christ.

6. *Nature declares that it is rational for one head to have one body.* Anything different is an abnormality, something contrary to natural law. In giving a simple but profound lesson, the Lord compared the church to a human body (I Cor. 12). Both man and the church have one head with one body consisting of many members. In the case of the church, Christ is the head (Eph. 1:22,23) and the members are the saved (Acts 2:47). By making this comparison the Bible appeals to reason, says there is as much sense in having one head with one body in the spiritual world as there is in the natural world. It would defy common sense for one head to have two or three hundred bodies with each fighting and seeking dominance over all the

others. But the Lord is not to blame and should not have to take the rap for man's irrationality.

7. *Jesus prayed that all who believed on Him through the Word might be one;* and then He stated a good reason for it, "That the world may believe that thou hast sent me" (Jno. 17:20,21). If unity promotes faith, as Jesus prayed, then division promotes infidelity.

8. "But what about *the churches of Christ* (Rom. 16:16)?" They were local churches or congregations. And "The seven churches which are in Asia" (Rev. 1:4) were local churches in Asia; their locations are given in chapters 2 and 3.

Once there was much prejudice against the "one church" idea; but today in the midst of an ecumenical atmosphere people are more nearly free of the former bias and the result is a growing perception. Reason is beginning to triumph.

SALVATION IN THE CHURCH

When a preacher asked a man why he did not become a church member, he was confounded with the answer: "If I can be saved out of the church as well as in it, why should I be in it?" The bewildered preacher mumbled a little, but it never made sense.

1. It makes sense for Jesus to have shed His blood for only *an essential institution* (Acts 20:28), for something you must be in to be saved. To have died for a church you can be saved out of as well as in is a gross absurdity.

2. Since Jesus bought the church with his blood, then logic says that for us *to be blood-bought we must be in the church.* So whatever one must do to get into the church that is what one must do to be cleansed by the blood.

Christ died for human redemption, for every creature in all

the world (Heb. 2:9). But His dying for a man is not enough to assure that person of redemption; if so, every person — not a single exception — would be redeemed. But the majority will be lost (Matt. 7:13,14), though Jesus died for them; so the redeemed are those who have met the conditions of blood-bought redemption, those who constitute the blood-bought church.

3. *Reconciliation unto God is in the one body or church:* "And that he might reconcile both [Jew and Gentile] unto God in one body by the cross" (Eph. 2:16). Therefore, reason tells us that if a person is not in the one body, then he has never been reconciled unto God.

4. *The church consists of the saved.* "The Lord added to the church daily such as should be saved" (Acts 2:47). So the church is the saved; and if a person could be saved out of it, he could be saved without belonging to the saved. Understandably, Jesus is the saviour of the church (Eph. 5:23). It is obvious, therefore, that the conditions of salvation and the conditions of church membership are the same, and in obeying one you obey the other.

5. *The house or family of God "is the church of the living God"* (I Tim. 3:15). So if He has children out of the church, then He has children out of His family — illegitimate ones. Perish the thought. This is unreasonable.

6. *If a person could be saved apart from the church,* he could be saved apart from Christ; for Christ is the head of the church (Eph. 1:22,23). However, Jesus declared that without or apart from Him "ye can do nothing" (Jno. 15:5). He appealed to man's reason, as He often did, in giving a common-sense illustration to enforce the thought, saying, "As the branch cannot bear fruit of itself, except it abide in the vine;

no more can ye, except ye abide in me" (Jno. 15:4). Jesus was so logical!

7. *Jesus will present the church unto Himself* at the last day (Eph. 5:27). Thus in order for one to be presented to the Lord when that great day comes, he must be in the church.

8. *Consistency does not tolerate half acceptance.* The idea, "I will take God but not Christ" is impossible. Just as ridiculous is the thought, "I will take Christ but not the church." If you accept God, you will have to accept His Son (Jno. 5:23); and if you accept the Son, you will have to accept His bride the church (II Cor. 11:2, Eph. 5:23). Reason bears out the idea that you cannot subscribe to the Bible in spots. The same authority that gave one verse gave all verses, so a rejection of any of it is a rejection of all of it (Jas. 2:10).

9. *Now a respondent explains,* "I believe Christ has a church; but it's the sects or denominations I can't swallow." It is understandable why you are not delighted with the schisms and isms of denominationalism. Because —

CHRIST'S CHURCH IS UNDENOMINATIONAL

1. *Denominationalism is antipodal to the principles of Christianity.*

(1) It divides the world into many religious bodies, while the Bible specifies one (Eph. 4:4).

(2) It frustrates mankind with many contradictory faiths, but the Bible pictures one (Eph. 4:5).

(3) In denominationalism there is the practice of many baptisms in contrast with the Biblical teaching of one (Eph. 4:5).

(4) Denominationalism mocks the prayer of Jesus for oneness (Jno. 17:20,21).

(5) In denominationalism there is the adherence to many contradictory rules, while the Bible says, "Let us walk by the same rule" (Phil. 3:16).

(6) Denominationalists work hard to make proselytes to their denomination, admitting that said membership is not essential to salvation. Their making unnecessary proselytes is like a work of the Pharisees, condemned by Jesus (Matt. 23;15).

(7) Paul condemned the spirit of denominationalism with sarcasm and ridicule. There were four groups at Corinth and three were wrong. Three were saying, "I am of Paul" — a Paulite; "I am of Apollos" — an Apollosite; "and I of Cephas" — a Cephasite. With stinging satire and divesting derision Paul asked, "Is Christ divided? was Paul crucified for you? or were ye baptized in the name of Paul" (I Cor. 1:12,13)? In other words, if Christ is not divided, why are you? If some man did not die for you, and if you were not baptized in his name, then why do you follow that man?

(8) Though some try, they cannot make a case for denominationalism from the Parable of the Vine and Branches (Jno. 15:1-6). However, they say, "The vine is the big church and the branches are denominations." But Jesus was not talking to denominations when He said, "I am the vine and ye are the branches." He was talking to men. He even said, ". . . a man . . . is . . . a branch," verse 6. Furthermore, it would be contrary to common sense to think that different kinds of branches grow on the same vine. Men do not "gather grapes of thorns, or figs of thistles" (Matt. 7:16).

2. *Now let us discern the undenominational unsectarian distinctions of the New Testament church.*

(1) No sectarian builder. Christ founded it (Matt. 16:18).

(2) No sectarian foundation. The rock upon which it was

founded is not Peter but the confession that Peter made that Jesus is the Son of God (Matt. 16:16-18; Eph. 2:20).

(3) No sectarian head. "Christ is the head of the church" (Eph. 5:23), the only head, visible and invisible.

(4) No sectarian confession. Upon becoming a member, one confesses that Jesus is the Son of God (Acts 8:36-38; Matt. 10:32). There is no confession of allegiance to church creeds or manuals or catechisms.

(5) No sectarian creed. The only creed is the Scriptures (II Tim. 3:16,17). No man has authority to enforce upon the church anything not taught in the Scriptures.

(6) No sectarian name. In fact, Christ's church has no special name. It is called (note the lack of capitals): "the church" (Acts 8:1); "church of God" (I Cor. 1:2); "churches of Christ," speaking of congregations (Rom. 16:16); "the body of Christ" (Eph. 4:12); "church of the living God" (I Tim. 3:15); and "church of the firstborn" Heb. 12:23).

The members are called "disciples" (Acts 20:7), "saints" (I Cor. 1:2), "beloved of God" (Rom. 1:7), "brethren" (I Cor. 15:6), "sons of God" (Rom. 8:14), "children of God" (I Jno. 3:1), "heirs of God" (Rom. 8:17) and "Christians" (Acts 11:26). The name *Christian* was given by the mouth of God, and is the fulfillment of the prophecy in Isa. 62:2. For it was a new name, one never worn before, and was given after the Gentiles had seen the righteousness of God (Acts 10), just as it was prophesied.

(7) No sectarian headquarters. There can be no earthly headquarters because each congregation is a self-governing group, independent of all other congregations.

The wisdom of this arrangement is clear. If one congregation becomes corrupted in doctrine or practice, others are not defiled. It is like a large window with many panes. If one pane is broken, it does not affect the others.

When you look at the scriptural attributes of Christ's church, you can see that there is no way you can classify it as a sectarian body or denomination.

3. *Hence, this appropriate question arises,* "Can a person today be a member of the same unsectarian church founded in Jerusalem, A.D. 33 (Acts 2)?" Yes! Certainly! This is possible because Christ's church can be restored anytime, in any community. The power to restore it is the word of God, the seed of the kingdom or church (Lk. 8:11). Everything produces after its own kind. Cotton produces cotton; corn produces corn; wheat produces wheat; and the word of God, the seed of the church, produces the church. The obeyed Word produced the church in Jerusalem (Acts 2). That same planted Word produced the church in Corinth: "I have planted, Apollos watered; but God gave the increase" (I Cor. 3:6). And that same unadulterated Word will produce the same church in any community today. For, in both nature and religion, "whatsoever a man soweth, that shall he also reap" (Gal. 6:7).

Here is an enlightening example: Barton W. Stone was a prominent preacher in a popular denomination in Kentucky. Because of a difference in doctrinal views he and some others were dismissed from it. At first they organized themselves into an independent presbytery, Springfield Presbytery. But about a year later they perceived that it was unscriptural, something unknown to the Bible. So in bringing about the death of what they had founded, they drew up the historic document, "The Last Will and Testament of the Springfield Presbytery," June 23, 1804. Here are some of the provisions of that will:

> (1) We will, that this body die, be dissolved and sink into union with the body of Christ at large. (2) We will

that our name of distinction, with its reverend title, be forgotten. (3) We will, that our power of making laws for the government of the church, executing them by delegated authority, forever cease. (4) We will that the church of Christ resume her native right of internal government. (5) We will, that the people henceforth take the Bible as their only guide.

This ended the denomination they had founded, and it is evident they did not establish a new one. What Stone and others did makes sense; and what they did we can do. By adhering to the slogan, "Speak where the Bible speaks, and be silent where the Bible is silent," we can bring rationality to a religious world cluttered and divided by the perversions of men.

REVIEW EXERCISE

1. How many churches did Jesus promise to build? ....
2. To how many churches did the Lord add the saved? ....
3. What did Jesus pray concerning unity? ....
4. The reconciliation made possible by the cross is found in.............. body.
5. Give five things wrong with denominationalism.

    (1) ....
    (2) ....
    (3) ....
    (4) ....
    (5) ....

6. How did Paul ridicule the spirit of denominationalism?...............
   ....

7. Why is it the Parable of the Vine and Branches cannot be used to support denominationalism? ....

....

8. Give six unsectarian characteristics of the church Jesus founded.

   (1) .... (2) ....

   (3) .... (4) ....

   (5) .... (6) ....

9. What is the unity spoken of in Jno. 10:16? ....

....

10. (T or F) There are as many divinely given bodies or churches as there are Gods.
11. Thought for discussion: Since the Lord adds the saved to the church, then there can be no saved people out of the church.
12. Thought for discussion: One cannot accept Christ without accepting His bride the church.

VIII

God's Plan of Salvation Is Sensible

GOD saves through Jesus Christ (Jno. 3:17). The death of Jesus is the sole meritorious cause of our salvation. "Christ died for our sins according to the Scriptures" (I Cor. 15:3).

BASIC THOUGHTS

1. *It was through Jesus that God reconciled the conflicting demands of justice and mercy.* There is an enlightening story handed down from the Medes and the Persians. A young man had put out both eyes of a fellow citizen. Justice, according to their rigid and inflexible law, required that two eyes be taken for the two he had destroyed. When the violator was brought to trial the judge was none other than his own father. In the heart of the judge there were the unyielding pulls of justice and mercy. Justice must be assessed but mercy must find a way. The father-judge pondered. The court was silent. Suspense ran high. Finally the judge lifted his bowed head and said, "As your judge, I can do no less than assess the full penalty of the law. Two eyes must be taken. But as your father, I offer one of my eyes to help meet the demands of justice."

Let us learn from the illustration. The whole accountable world was guilty of sin (Rom. 3:23). Sin is wrong. It separates man from God (Isa. 59:2). Justice cries out for sin to be punished (Rom. 6:23). But mercy cries out for man's pardon. So God sent His Son to resolve the discordant claims of justice and grace. "To wit, that God was in Christ, reconciling the world unto himself, not imputing their trespasses unto them; and hath committed unto us the word of reconciliation" (II Cor. 5:19). The Son's power to bring it about, as seen in the verse, is in the Word — "the word of reconciliation" — or the gospel, which suggests that the Word gives a plan for man to obey. What man does is merely appropriative.

2. *Salvation is either conditional or unconditional;* if unconditional, everybody would be saved. For God "will have all men to be saved, and to come unto the knowledge of the truth" (I Tim. 2:3,4). If any are lost, it is not God's fault but theirs, all because they have not met the divine terms of pardon.

3. *Man cannot have pardon on his own terms.* If he can, then the whole world is guilty of nonsense; for courts the world over say that the law violator can obtain pardon only by meeting the specified terms of pardon. That is common sense. No criminal can say, "I've rectified my breach of the law by forgiving myself. Now I'm free." Nor can he say, "I don't care what the law says. I've decided to pardon myself by doing so and so."

But when it comes to spiritual pardon, the disregard of this common sense principle is widespread. The prevalence of this irrationality in Habakkuk's day caused him to write: "Their judgment and their dignity shall proceed of themselves" (Hab. 1:7). Their judgment or justice proceeded from themselves, from their own ideas and opinions. Many people think God feels the way they do because they think God is like themselves. This basic error was mentioned by the Psalmist: "Thou thoughtest that I was altogether such an one as thyself" (Psa. 50:21). Since many people think they can be saved by morality alone, or by faith only, or by any other way they wish, it is easy for them to think that God feels the same way. But common sense tells us that if God does the pardoning, He has the right to set the conditions. To try to be saved some other way is but to dishonor the God whose forgiveness we seek. That is appalling.

4. *Concerning those that are lost* — their not obeying the gospel is not the cause of it. They were already lost; *they are lost because of sin*. Their not obeying the gospel is the cause of their not being saved, for "the gospel is the power of God unto salvation" (Rom. 1:16). "God sent not his Son into the world to condemn the world [the world was already condemned because of sin]; but that the world through him might be saved" (Jno. 3:17). Christ's coming and giving the saving gospel leaves the sinner without excuse. Jesus said, "If I had not come and spoken unto them, they had not had sin [the sin of rejecting Him]; but now they have no cloak [excuse] for their sin" (Jno. 15:22), no excuse for not being forgiven.

DIVINE PLAN OF SALVATION FOR THE UNREDEEMED

Several distinct lines of reasoning bring us to the same conclusion:

1. *The gospel of Christ saves those who believe it and obey it:* "The gospel of Christ . . . is the power of God unto salvation to everyone that believeth" (Rom. 1:16). But to believe only in it will not suffice, for Jesus will come in flaming fire and take "vengeance on them that know not God, and that obey not the gospel" (II Thess. 1:7-9).

But what is the gospel? Paul declared that the gospel is that Christ died for our sins according to the Scriptures; and that he was buried, and that he rose again the third day according to the Scriptures" (I Cor. 15:1-4).

But how can one obey the death, burial and resurrection of Christ? Paul tells us how. He tells us to obey the *form* of it: "Ye have obeyed from the heart that form of doctrine which was delivered you. Being then made free from sin [after obedience to the form of doctrine] ye became the servants of righteousness" (Rom. 6:17,18). We obey from the heart the form of it by dying to sin (repentance) and by being buried in a watery grave (immersion) and by being raised to walk in newness of life. Paul explicitly states this in Rom. 6:3,4: "Therefore we are buried with him by baptism into death: that like as Christ was raised up from the dead by the glory of the Father, even so we also should walk in newness of life."

Here we see the wisdom of God in appointing immersion for baptism instead of some other act. It is a figure of the death, burial and resurrection of our Saviour, and as such is a silent witness to these blessed facts. "There are three that bear witness on earth," and one of them is water — baptism (I Jno. 5:8). Thus God planned for baptism to be something declarative and meaningful. What the burial in water (immersion) symbolizes will not permit a substitute. Some other references are Col. 2:12; Matt. 3:13-16; Acts 8:36-38.

2. *One must be born again:* "Except a man be born again, he cannot see the kingdom of God" (Jno. 3:3). Jesus is talking about being *born again,* a *new* birth — not the first birth. And He is talking about a *man's* being born again — not the birth of an unborn child. The man He addressed was puzzled as to how this could occur. Jesus explained the new birth in verse 5, saying, "Except a man be born of water and of the Spirit, he cannot enter into the kingdom of God." That is the new birth — birth of water and the Spirit.

A person is born of or begotten of the Spirit as the Spirit operates through the Word to quicken him. Peter said so: "Being born again, not of corruptible seed, but of incorruptible, by the word of God, which liveth and abideth for ever" (I Pet. 1:23). And James declared the same, "Of his own will begat he us with the word of truth" (Jas. 1:18). The Spirit gave the Word (II Pet. 1:21), and thereby uses a fair and understandable medium to beget lost souls into the new birth. This shows the reasonableness and equity of God. It would be unintelligible and unfair for man's new birth to depend on some inexplainable agency that floats through the air, hits one and misses another. However, in God's plan for the new birth, begotten by the Word, there is man's part in the process which is to believe the Word and obey it. Never underrate its power when believed; for it is "the word of God, which effectually worketh also in you that believe" (I Thess. 2:13). For one to be blessed, it must work obedience in his life (Jas. 1:22).

To be *born of water* means to be baptized. In birth a person comes into a new life; in baptism a person is raised to a new life (Rom. 6:34; Col. 2:12); they are equal, for things equal to the same thing are equal to each other. "Born of water" is more evidence for immersion, for no person can be born of a substance less than himself.

3. *An alien's becoming a citizen is informative:* A German citizen hears of the United States of America. He believes what he hears. As a result he turns his back on his old country and comes to America. Still he is not a citizen, just an alien. He confesses allegiance to America, and in a final and culminating act he becomes a citizen of the United States.

In similar fashion a person becomes a citizen of Christ's kingdom. Prior to this he is an alien, described by Paul: "That at that time ye were without Christ, being aliens from the commonwealth of Israel, and strangers from the covenants of promise, having no hope, and without God in the world" (Eph. 2:12). The alien hears of Christ and His kingdom, an absolute necessity: "how shall they believe in him of whom they have not heard" (Rom. 10:14)? As a result, he believes in the Lord and His kingdom: "So then faith cometh by hearing, and hearing by the word of God" (Rom. 10:17). His working faith (Gal. 5:6) moves him to turn his back upon his old relationship, to repent (Acts 2:38). He confesses faith in Christ (Rom. 10:10; I Jno. 4:15). And in a terminal act of becoming a citizen he is baptized into Christ (Rom. 6:3,4).

This must make sense. For the U.S. follows these parallel steps in admitting aliens into citizenship.

4. *There is no surer way,* however, to learn "what must I do to be saved" than to go to each place the question is asked and read the answer. Substantially, the question is asked only four times in the New Testament, and one of them was under the law of Moses. It was propounded by the rich young man who came to Jesus (Mk. 10:17). Jesus referred him to the Ten Commandments because the Mosaic law was in force at this time, for Christ had not yet died and nailed it to the cross (Col. 2:14). But Jesus saw something else lacking and said, "One thing thou lackest: go thy way, sell whatsoever thou hast, and give to the poor, and thou shalt have treasure in heaven: and come, take up the cross, and follow me." The rich young man needed to free himself of his riches because in his case they were a stumbling block; additionally he was directed to follow Christ, for this would better train him for work in the coming Christian dispensation. This answer would not be given today because it was before the New Testament became effective (Heb. 9:16,17).

After the New Testament went into effect, the question was asked three times: and three different answers were given, though all did exactly the same things.

Question one: "Men and brethren, what shall we do (Acts 2:37)? *The answer:* "Repent and be baptized every one of you in the name of Jesus Christ for the remission of sins . . ." (Acts 2:38). They were not told to believe because they had already believed, so much that they asked what to do. Hence, they were told only to repent and to be baptized.

Question two: "Lord, what wilt thou have me to do" (Acts 9:6)? *The answer:* "Arise, and go into the city, and it shall be told thee what thou must do" (Acts 9:6). In the city he was told: "Arise, and be baptized, and wash away thy sins, calling on the name of the Lord" (Acts 22:16). He was not told to believe and repent because he had already done this. He believed so much that he was ready to forsake his Jewish religion and asked what to do; he was so penitent that for three days and nights he neither ate nor slept. So he was told to do what he had not done — to be baptized.

Question three: "Sirs, what must I do to be saved" (Acts 16:30)? *The answer:* "Believe on the Lord Jesus Christ, and thou shalt be saved, and thy house" (Acts 16:31). This question was asked by a man who had never heard the gospel and thus did not believe. So he was told to believe but not to believe only. (When Paul spoke of salvation by faith, as he did here and in Rom. 5:1, he meant an obedient faith. He said, "obedience to the faith," Rom. 1:5 and "the obedience of faith," Rom. 16:26. Any other degree of faith is to no avail, Jno. 12:48.) Then Paul preached to the man that he might believe and he repented (his washing Paul's stripes was the fruit of repentance) and was baptized the same hour of the night (Acts 16:33). Hence, he believed, repented and was baptized, as each did in every case. All did exactly the same things.

As an example, a gentleman asks how far is it to Chicago. The answer is nine hundred miles. He drives three hundred miles and asks the same question. Now he is told that it is six hundred. He drives three hundred miles farther and asks the question again. This time the answer is three hundred. He was given three different answers to the same question, because he was at different places on the road to Chicago.

Now let us apply the same common sense to the question of salvation. The inquirers were at different places on the road to forgiveness. The *first* had believed, so they were told to repent and be baptized. The *second* had believed and repented, and was told to be baptized. The *third* had never started on the road, so in a blanket way he was told to believe (meaning an obedient belief) and then they preached to him that he might believe and he repented and was baptized. All traveled over the same road. All did the same things. There is no contradiction here.

LAW OF PARDON FOR THE ERRING CHILD OF GOD

The saved person — born again — can sin. John (a strong Christian) said, "If we say that we have no sin, we deceive ourselves, and the truth is not in us" (I Jno. 1:8). Accordingly, reason tells us that there must be some means of forgiveness for God's erring child; furthermore, it tells us that this law must be different from the conditions given the alien. The child of God who sins is not an alien — errant but not an alien; therefore the law of pardon to him must not be that given to the alien. God made this distinction, and adapted a suitable law to each.

Fortunately for us, the two laws are found side by side in the Bible and are very discernible. We read of a man who believed and was baptized (Acts 8:13), and according to Jesus he was saved (Mk. 16:16). Later he sinned by trying to buy the gift of God with money (Acts 8:18-21). Now what shall he do to obtain pardon? Believe and be baptized again? No. He was told: "Repent therefore of this thy wickedness, and pray God, if perhaps the thought of thine heart may be forgiven thee" (Acts 8:22). While this passage does not specifically mention confession of sin (of course true repentance compels it), other passages do: "If we confess our sins, he is faithful and just to forgive us our sins, and to cleanse us from all unrighteousness" (I Jno. 1:9). Also, Jas. 5:16. Reason tells us that the confession of sin should surely be as wide as it is known in order to remove the stumbling block it has become.

The sensibleness of God's laws of pardon to the alien and to the erring is most apparent. How workable and practical each is!

REVIEW EXERCISE

1. What is the sole meritorious cause of our salvation? ....
   ....

2. What does justice require of sin? ....
   What does mercy cry out? ....

3. What is the "word of reconciliation?" ....
   ....

4. How does Hab. 1:7 describe many people today? ....
   ....

5. What causes people to be lost? ....
   What enables them to be saved? ....

6. How can one obey the death, burial and resurrection of Christ?
   ....

7. How can one be born again? ....
   ....

8. How does an alien's becoming a citizen of U.S. illustrate an alien sinner's becoming a citizen in God's kingdom? ....
   ....

9. What were believing people on Pentecost told to do to be saved?
   ....

10. What was Saul told to do to be saved? ....
    ....

11. Why was the jailer told just to believe to be saved? ....
    ....

12. Explain that there is no contradiction in the three different answers to the question of salvation. ....
    ....
    ....

IX

The Common Sense of Christian Growth

NOW that one has been born again — become a Christian — what do Scripture and common sense (for they go together) tell us should be his lifestyle for the rest of his days?

The answer is found in the sensible comment of a native chief in a distant land. He said to a missionary, "I don't object to my people's becoming Christians, provided they become good Christians." Anything less than a good one is inconsistent with the calling.

GROWTH IS SENSIBLE

1. *The new birth demands a new life.* From the waters of baptism one is raised to "walk in newness of life" (Rom. 6:3,4). Being now a new creature, it is only reasonable that God demand that the old life be laid aside and that all things become new (II Cor. 5:17).

Of course, the world is still filled with evil, the flesh is still flesh and temptation is still a realistic threat. Even Jesus suffered temptations after He was baptized (Matt. 4:1-11).

2. Children of God may sin (I Jno. 1:8-2:2); because *the new life, following the new birth, is not a state of perfection but rather a state of growth.* Be not dismayed that you were not born full grown. It would be contrary to common sense. Furthermore, it would leave a person with no room for improvement, which is the role of deity — not human beings. If the infant should have been born an adult, it would rob him of

the joy of growing. Likewise, if the newborn creature were born full grown, it would leave him without a challenge and destitute of one of life's greatest joys and appeals — that of pursuing.

> Let us, then, be up and doing,
> With a heart for any fate;
> Still achieving, still pursuing,
> Learn to labor and to wait.
> — Henry Wadsworth Longfellow

Years after becoming a Christian, Paul was still pursuing and working at self-control. He freely stated: "Brethren, I count not myself to have apprehended" (Phil. 3:13).

3. *The common sense of nature has established the law of growth.* A little plant breaks the surface of the earth and starts lifting itself toward the sky until it becomes grown and then begins to gradually fade. An animal is born and progresses until it becomes mature and then there is a gradual retrogression of strength and stamina. A man is born into the world a baby and naturally grows until he is grown, and then old age slowly but surely begins to develop.

4. *However, there is one kind of growth in which there should be no anti-climax,* and this is spiritual or Christian growth. "Though our outward man perish, yet the inward man is renewed day by day" (II Cor. 4:16). It is God's wise plan for the physical man to grow until he reaches full strength and then start gradually dying, for this body must be left behind (II Cor. 5:1). And it is just as wise for the spiritual man to grow and grow a lifetime, for this is the man that is to continue, clothed in a new body (Phil. 3:21), in another world forever.

5. There is as much sense in *the urgency of growth for the newborn babe in Christ* as there is for the firstborn infant.

A failure to grow physically or spiritually opposes the law of God.

A little child fell out of bed one night. It scared him and he began to cry. The mother rushed into the room, took him into her arms and asked, "Sonny, what happened?" "Mommy, I guess I went to sleep too close to where I got in." This is the fault of many who entered salvation. They went to sleep too close to where they got in. It is contrary to Scripture and reason.

NEGATIVE CONDITIONS OF GROWTH

The apostle Peter is very explicit in stating both negatively and positively some of the prerequisites of development:

> Wherefore laying aside all malice, and all guile, and hypocrisies, and envies, and all evil speakings, as newborn babes, desire the sincere milk of the word, that ye may grow thereby: if so be ye have tasted that the Lord is gracious.
>
> — I Peter 2:1-3

Having been regenerated to a new life by the power of the word of God (I Pet. 1:23), it is incumbent upon the new convert to lay aside everything that impedes spiritual growth and particularly that which corrupts a pure heart and interferes with a fervent love of the brethren (I Pet. 1:22). The apostle specifies five evils that are to be laid aside:

1. *Lay aside malice.* The original word is evil of any kind, but in this setting it indicates an evil and wicked disposition that seeks to injure another. Being bent on doing harm to others is antagonistic to the spirit of love. For one to grow in Christian service, there must prevail in his heart the spirit of returning good for evil (I Thess. 5:15; I Pet. 3:9).

2. *Put away all guile.* Lay aside deceit. Do not use bait

or craftiness to attain wishes. The Pharisees did some good things *per se* but out of ulterior motives from guileful hearts, which redounded to their condemnation (Matt. 23:5). The reason for doing a thing is as important as the act itself.

3. *Lay aside all hypocrisies.* Two-faced actions and double dealings are not Christian. The religion of the Pharisees, however, was a game of pretense calculated to fool others. Their hypocrisies were aptly described by Jesus in five words: "They say, and do not" (Matt. 23:3). If we would grow in beauty and goodness, we must be sincere.

4. *Put away envies.* These are the feelings of dissatisfaction and frustration over another's success because one sees in the other person what he would like to be or have. The envious person ordinarily pursues a course of tearing down another in the sinful and futile effort of trying to build himself up. It is his wicked way of trying to even up the status quo. Behind a lot of "church" troubles you will find envy.

In the woods I once examined a fallen tree. It was easy to see what caused it to fall, wither and die. It was rotten on the inside. It fell under the stress of a little wind, but it was not the wind that caused it to fall. It fell because it had weakened itself on the inside. No person can grow by following a course that destroys him on the inside, and envy does — "envy the rottenness of the bones" (Prov. 14:30).

5. *Lay aside all evil speakings:* slanders and defamatory remarks about others. This word is translated *backbitings* in II Cor. 12:20. *Backknifings.* Do not do to another's back what you would not do to his face. The Bible declares that a slanderer is a fool (Prov. 10:18). Common sense says the same. How foolish to steal from another that which does not enrich the thief!

> Who steals my purse steals trash; 'tis
> something, nothing;
> 'Twas mine, 'tis his, and has been slave
> to thousands;
> But he that filches from me my good name
> Robs me of that which not enriches him,
> And makes me poor indeed.
> — William Shakespeare

POSITIVE REQUIREMENTS OF GROWTH

We have observed some of the Holy Spirit's *negatives* for growth; now let us note some *positives* — things we are obliged to do:

1. *The newborn person must have food.* The right kind. And sufficient amounts. Peter says, "Desire the sincere milk of the word that ye may grow thereby." Nature says no material food, no material growth. And just as sensible, the Bible says no spiritual food, no spiritual growth.

I have seen pictures of little bodies with big swollen stomachs, the victims of malnutrition. But even more pitiable are some starved children of God with big heads and shriveled souls. The Lord provided the diet — the milk of the Word and the meat of the Word (Heb. 5:12-14) — but they have not eaten.

There is the story of a farmer who began whipping his half-starved horse for weakening at the plow. A passer-by said, "Instead of whipping him, why don't you feed him?" The lesson is clear to the church.

2. *Exercise is an absolute necessity.* It is as necessary for the spiritual man as it is for the physical man. "Exercise thyself rather unto godliness. For bodily exercise profiteth little [for a little time]: but godliness is profitable unto all things, having promise of the life that now is, and of that which is to come" (I Tim. 4:7,8).

There must be exercises unto godliness — do some things, engage in positives. While the Christian is to refrain from the works of the flesh (Gal. 5:19-21), he must also produce the fruit of the Spirit (Gal. 5:22,23). Christianity is a religion of more than denials.

Here are some spiritual exercises that stimulate growth:

(1) Teach and win lost souls. The convert is to be taught to do what Jesus taught the apostles, one of which acts is to go teach and baptize the lost (Matt. 28:19,20). So the command to teach stands enjoined upon every baptized believer. In this exercise — winning another to the Lord — is found a major cause for the individual and collective growth of the members of the early church: "They that were scattered abroad went everywhere preaching the word" (Acts 8:4). No wonder they had additions daily (Acts 2:47). If Christianity is worth embracing, it is worth sharing with others.

(2) Pray (Col. 4:2). Talking matters over with God in a spirit of reverence, faith, penitence and openness is bound to be helpful. Furthermore, God answers prayer (I Jno. 5:14). Just you and God can do a lot for you.

(3) Comfort the bereaved: ". . . comfort one another with these words" (I Thess. 4:18). Express the sympathetic spirit.

(4) Encourage the fainthearted. Jesus had compassion on the multitudes because they fainted, were distressed (Matt. 9:36). A little sunshine of concern from you will help drive away their clouds. "Bear ye one another's burdens" is sensible, practical religion (Gal. 6:2).

(5) Greet strangers. This matter will come up at the judgment (Matt. 25:35,38). Strangers are often bewildered. They need help to get adjusted in a new location. Visit them. Ask them to visit you.

(6) Visit the sick. This is another duty that will be tested at the judgment (Matt. 25:36,39). Do not wait until you have suffered a spell of illness to see the need of it.

(7) Be forgiving. God is and if we are not, then we are not godly. Devoid of this quality, we are not on praying terms with God: "Forgive us our debts, as we forgive our debtors" (Matt. 6:12). Not just seven times but seventy times seven (Matt. 18:22). The more we grow, the easier it is to forgive.

(8) Exercise your senses to discern good and evil (Heb. 5:14). Learn the difference between man's custom and God's law. Be not swept away from truth by majority opinion (Ex. 23:2). Be your own person. Decide what is right and stand for it.

(9) "Follow after the things which make for peace" (Rom. 14:19). You must if you would be blessed (Matt. 5:9).

(10) Assist the needy (Eph. 4:28). This exercise enlarges the heart and makes a bigger person. While the destitute are blessed by your benevolence, you are blessed more (Acts 20:35). Try it and you will see.

(11) "As we have therefore opportunity, let us do good unto all men" (Gal. 6:10). This exercise will shape you more into the image of the Christ "who went about doing good": (Acts 10:38). If you keep your eyes open, the opportunities will come; and as you seize them, you will grow.

(12) Concerning our religion toward others, it has been formulated and compacted into just one short statement, known as the Golden Rule, which calls for *doing:* "Therefore all things whatsoever ye would that men should do to you, do ye even so to them" (Matt. 7:12).

(13) Summed up, whatever pertains to the life that God has prescribed for man — consecration, work and worship — this

is godliness, and man should exercise himself in the cultivation and performance of it.

3 *Freedom from disease is essential to growth.* Spiritually, we call it sin, for sin is the disease of the soul. It can check and kill spiritual development. Watch and pray that you enter not into temptation (Matt. 26:4). If you should sin, repent and pray for God's forgiveness (Acts 8:22). Then leave it behind (Phil. 3:13,14).

4 *Keep yourself in a favorable environment.* Just as climate may affect physical growth, environment may affect spiritual growth. "Be not deceived: evil communications [companionships] corrupt good manners [morals]" (I Cor. 15:33). In the presence of some people it is easy to do right, but in the company of others it is more difficult. Peter learned this the hard way by warming at the devil's fire, lighted and kindled by the wrong crowd (Mk. 14:54, 66-72). If he had been with a different crowd, the chances are he would not have denied Jesus.

5. *Time is required.* "For when for the time ye ought to be teachers" (Heb. 5:12). It is a lifetime program, so do not expect to become mature in a day. Every day, however, is important and may add a little to your development. Like growing physically, you cannot see it each day; but after time has passed, you can look back and see that you have grown.

Assuming that you are meeting the requirements of growth, you are becoming a bigger child of God. You are enlarging in "stature of the fulness of Christ" (Eph. 4:13). You are growing "up into him in all things" (Eph. 4:15).

REVIEW EXERCISE

1. Give two Scriptures which speak of a new life or new creature.

....

2. What is the one kind of growth in which there should be no anticlimax? ....
3. What does nature say about the sensibleness of growth? ....
....
4. List five negative conditions of Christian growth. (1) ....
.... (2) .... (3) ....
(4) .... (5) ....
5. What is the food for the newborn person in Christ? ....
6. What exercise did Paul say "profiteth little?" ....
7. What is the exercise that is "profitable unto all things?" ....
....
8. What is the short statement that describes our religion toward others? ....
9. What did Paul say that the wrong environment or companionship can do to us? ....
10. What should the newborn Christian be able to do after time has passed? ....
11. Thought question: Is it any more reasonable to expect one to be born full grown spiritually than it is to expect him to be born full grown physically?
12. Thought question: What are some spiritual exercises we can do that are not listed in lesson?

X
Worship Is Sensible

IF God be the creator of man — and He is — then it is sensible for man to worship Him; to refuse, represses a natural instinct and defies the common practices of all peoples of all ages. For worship is as old as man and as universal as his existence. It is apparent that man *is* a religious creature, that he will worship; however blindly, he will worship.

Man's kinship with God, together with the recognition of his entire dependence upon God, impels him to pay homage to God and to seek communion with Him. This universal feeling has been intelligently and beautifully expressed by the psalmist: "O come, let us worship and bow down: let us kneel before the Lord our maker" (Psa. 95:6).

WORSHIP IS DUE THE LORD

In another passage the psalmist said:

> Give unto the Lord the glory due unto his name; worship the Lord in the beauty of holiness.
>
> — Psalms 29:2

There are good sensible reasons for it which we shall consider.

1. *Six reasons are spelled out in one passage:* "Serve the Lord with gladness: come before his presence with singing. Know ye that the Lord he is God: it is he that hath made us, and not we ourselves; we are his people, and the sheep of his pasture. Enter into his gates with thanksgiving, and into his courts with praise: be thankful unto him, and bless his name. For the Lord is good; his mercy is everlasting; and his truth

endureth to all generations" (Psa. 100:2-5). These reasons are specified in the text for worshiping God:

(1) "He is God." When you accept this thesis, worship is a natural consequence.

(2) "He hath made us." The product should glorify the maker.

(3) "We are his people." That relationship carries the privilege and obligation of worship.

(4) "The Lord is good." We are inclined to pay homage to the extraordinary, the good and the great. None qualifies like God.

(5) "His mercy is everlasting." This impels worship. Drinking from His cup of mercy swells the heart in natural and unlabored praise.

(6) "His truth endureth." The enduring nature of God, His mercy and truth, shows where our worship should be focused.

God alone is worthy of worship. Jesus said, "Thou shalt worship the Lord thy God, and him only shalt thou serve" (Matt. 4:10). In the verse Jesus recognized worship and service as separate entities but He tied them together. Wherever you have one the other naturally follows. Whatever else you may be tempted to worship and serve — money, ambition, personal standing, fleshly appetite, beauty, ease, affection and friends — all of them, one by one, shall disappear. But God remains, unaffected, unchanged. By worshiping Him we stay closer to Him. Truly, a strong bulwark of safety in the midst of dangers is worship.

2. *Another passage gives four more sound reasons for worship:* "Bless the Lord, O my soul: and all that is within me, bless his holy name. Bless the Lord, O my soul, and forget

not all his benefits . . . He hath not dealt with us after our sins; nor rewarded us according to our iniquities . . . Like as a father pitieth his children, so the Lord pitieth them that fear him. For he knoweth our frame; he remembereth that we are dust" (Psa. 103:1-14). These are the well-advised reasons given in the text for worship:

(1) "His benefits." Because of divinely provided benefits we should "bless the Lord, O my soul." "Every good gift and every perfect gift is from above, and cometh down from the Father . . ." (Jas. 1:17). So we ask, "What shall I render unto the Lord for all his benefits toward me" (Psa. 116:12)? The answer is *worship* and *service*. May we not live like the hogs that eat the acorns under the trees without ever looking up to see from whence they come.

(2) "He hath not dealt with us according to our sins." He has dealt with us on the basis of a mercy that has provided the way whereby our sins may be forgiven rather than punished. He does not want us to be lost (I Tim. 2:3,4).

(3) Like a father, "the Lord pitieth them that fear him." His pity is vividly and touchingly portrayed in the parable of the Prodigal Son (Lk. 15:11-32). The intelligence of the whole world says that just as the father has a duty to the child, the child has a duty to the father. In this case -- worship.

(4) "He knoweth our frame [its weakness] . . . that we are dust." We are weak. God is strong. As we worship Him we become stronger, for we tend to become like what we worship. Every passing moment of worship has a molding effect upon us, however minute, in the likeness of God.

3. *Two more sensible reasons for worship* are stated in Psa. 138:2,3:

(1) "Thou hast magnified thy word." Magnified it in *practi-*

cality. It meets man's needs. Magnified it in *truth.* Every word is true. Magnified it in *promises.* He keeps His word. "The Lord is not slack concerning his promise" (II Pet. 3:9). We can count on His word. Let us praise Him for it.

(2) "Thou answeredst me, and strengthenest me with strength in my soul." This is where man needs strength the most — in the soul. And it may be derived from worship. "No man can serve two masters" (Matt. 6:24). The more a person makes God the master of his soul and the object of his worship, the more he pulls away from Satan (Jas. 4:7,8). Give God your devotion and He shall give you strength. The very nature of worship — the consciousness of God, the pouring out of self in homage, the humility, the self-examination, the adoration of Him who is perfect, the expression of praise and the disposition to please — is sure to lift man and give him a sense of truer direction.

PUBLIC WORSHIP

1. In the light of the foregoing it is understandable why *public worship has been customarily and regularly observed.* There is too much to gain from it to wilfully miss it.

(1) Christ customarily attended public worship: "As his custom was, he went into the synogogue on the sabbath day, and stood up for to read" (Lk. 4:16). This was not an occasional function but a customary practice. It occurred on the Sabbath and in the synogogue, because the Jewish law was still in force and remained until the death of Christ (Col. 2:14).

(2) However, after the New Testament dispensation became effective, the early disciples attended public worship upon the first day of the week: "And upon the first day of the week, when the disciples came together to break bread, Paul preached unto them . . ." (Acts 20:7). *Which* first day of the week?

There is but one. There never has been a week without a first day or with more than one. Hence, it was not necessary to say *every* first day of the week, no more than it was necessary to say, "Remember every sabbath day." It sufficed to say, "Remember the sabbath" (Ex. 20:8), because every week had a Sabbath.

The Corinthian church was commanded to contribute on the first day of the week (I Cor. 16:2). It does not say *every first day* but it teaches it, for every week has a first day. The command implies that they assembled. And definite proof of their assembling is seen in I Cor. 11:20: "When ye come together therefore into one place . . ."

(3) The early church was commanded to not forsake the public assembly: "Not forsaking the assembling of ourselves together, as the manner of some is" (Heb. 10:25). Some had. In so doing, they violated a command of God and common sense. It was a sin of omission (Jas. 4:17).

2. *Public worship involves the local church* which is another arrangement from the intelligence of God. That it existed is most evident. There are letters in the New Testament to local churches. Also, qualifications are given for elders and deacons in the local church. And it is there that discipline is exercised (Matt. 18:17), leadership is maintained (Heb. 13:17), cooperative work is exerted (II Cor. 6:1) and cooperative worship is offered unto God. Of course, man can work and worship privately, but cooperative work and worship are also for his good and the carrying out of a necessary part of God's plan.

Man's banding together in a common cause in units or groups is sound reasoning. What would you think of Rotarians, Kiwanians and Lions if they had no club organization and never assembled, if each just followed the principles of such privately? Neither would last long. Likewise, to think that Christianity can be maintained without the public assembly of worship is sheer nonsense.

3. *Public worship shows:*

(1) A purpose to worship, for it provides a set time and place for it.

(2) A disposition to obey a command of God, for it is commanded.

(3) Our faith, for we demonstrate our faith by our works (Jas. 2:18).

(4) Our love, for we prove our love by obeying the commandments (Jno. 14:15).

In a woman's insupportable excuse for not going to church, she said, "I don't have to go to church on Sunday. I have a seven-day-a-week religion — not just on Sunday." Frankly, if she has, it would include Sunday. But on that day her religion is so meaningless that she wilfully violates a command of God.

4. *Nonattendance is hurting the church.* Of course, worship requires more than occupying a pew. Christianity will not settle for a mere pew-sitter and lip-server. However, every knowledgeable, fair minded person will freely admit that absenteeism is today one of the most ravaging enemies of religion.

ACTS OF PUBLIC WORSHIP

Worship is the paying of divine honor, religious homage and venerable devotion in formal acts of the mind. It has to be in the form of some thought or act, controlled by man's mind or heart. Call it rites, call it ceremonies, call it what you will, but reason declares that something must occur in worship.

Consequently, there are five items of worship mentioned in the New Testament, each of which is a separate act that is sensible and needful:

1. *Prayer.* With soul devout, prayer puts one in conversation with God. Conscious of one's own frailty, he commits himself to God, saying, "Thy will be done in earth, as it is in heaven" (Matt. 6:10). An uplifting experience.

Paul instructed the disciples to give thanks along with their petitions to God (Phil. 4:6). Unless we are thankful for what we have received, we are not spiritually qualified to ask for more.

Prayer demands a genuineness and sincerity, devoid of which it rings with a mockery that will eventually force a change of attitude or dry up the praying. In Samuel Taylor Coleridge's *Rime of the Ancient Mariner* we have the poetic presentation of how sin hinders prayer:

> I looked to heaven, and tried to pray
> But or ever a prayer had gusht,
> A wicked whisper came, and made
> My heart as dry as dust.

2. *Singing.* When a congregation of worshipers sing together, speak to themselves and to God in psalms and hymns and spiritual songs, the heart swells in a recollection of past events, in an expression of present convictions, and in rekindling of hopes for the future. It is sure to help!

In our songs we praise God. Also, in songs we teach and admonish one another (Col. 3:16). This can be effected only through an expression of words, which can be better carried out if nothing clashes with or destroys the sound and the articulation.

Here are the passages giving the record of vocal music in

the New Testament: Matt. 26:30; Acts 16:25; Rom. 15:9; Cor. 14:15; Eph. 5:19; Col. 3:16; Heb. 2:12; Heb. 13:15; Jas. 5:13. They make an interesting study, what they say and — especially what they do not say.

3. *Preaching and teaching.* If the Word will do for us what we profess, then it makes sense for us to be taught it (Acts 20: 7,32; II Tim. 3:16,17).

4. *The Lord's Supper.* The early church engaged in this item of worship as a sweet and sacred memorial on the first day of the week (I Cor. 11:23-29). It makes sense. For there is nothing that memoralizes as effectively as the Lord's Supper. Not the rainbow (Gen. 9:13-17). Not a statue. Not a lock of hair in the Bible. We need this designated period of weekly remembrance, for it is so easy to forget (Jer. 2:32).

5. *Contribution.* The intelligence of all peoples of all religions say that it is rational to sacrifice to your god. The early Christians continued steadfastly in giving or fellowship (Acts 2:42). The common sense of Christ's religion is especially evident in the command to give, I Cor. 16:2: (1) *The regularity* — "Upon the first day of the week." (2) *The givers* — "let every one of you." This is fair and reasonable. (3) *The act* — "lay by him in store." (4) *The amount* — "as God hath prospered him." He who makes more should give more. Nothing is more sensible. Our government follows this principle in taxing the people. (5) *The elimination of erratic, hodgepodge financing* — "that there be no gatherings when I come."

How sensible is worship! Every item of it! How nonsensical to neglect it!

REVIEW EXERCISE

1. What postures are related to worship, as stated in Psa. 95:6?

....

2. What question is asked in Psalms concerning the benefits we receive from the Lord? ....

3. Give four blessings in Psa. 103:1-14 that should make us want to worship God. (1) .... (2) ....
 .... (3) .... (4) ....

4. How do we prove that the early disciples attended public worship on the first day of the week? ....
....

5. What were the early Christians told to not forsake? ....
....

6. Give the five items of public worship. (1) ....
 (2) .... (3) ....
 (4) .... (5) ....

7. (T or F) Jesus related worship and service.
8. (T or F) Christ felt no need to attend public worship.
9. (T or F) The same phraseology that describes the regularity of taking the Lord's Supper is used to describe the regularity of giving.
10. (T or F) The Lord deals with us strictly according to our sins.
11. Thought for discussion: Absenteeism from public worship is hurting the church.
12. Thought for discussion: It would be difficult to maintain the local church without public worship.

XI
Common Sense at Random in the Scriptures

As further proof of the sensibleness of God's religion we call attention to a number of Scriptures at random:

MISCELLANEOUS SCRIPTURES

1. *The essentiality of connection.* "As the branch cannot bear fruit of itself, except it abide in the vine [every one sees the sensibleness of this]; no more can ye, except ye abide in me" (Jno. 15:4). Reason says that a branch must have a life-sustaining connection with the vine; and as equally logical, man must have a connection with Jesus who is "the way, the truth, and the life" (Jno. 14:6). For without Him we can do nothing (Jno. 15:5).

2. *Count the cost.* "For which of you, intending to build a tower, sitteth not down first, and counteth the cost, whether he have sufficient to finish it" (Lk. 14:28)? This is sensible. To fail in counting the cost may force you to leave an unfinished building that is impractical and embarrassing. The same common sense should be drawn upon in becoming a Christian. Count the cost. The reward is worth more than the whole world, but a price has to be paid. To begin and quit puts one in a worse condition than he was beforehand (II Pet. 2:20-22).

3. *Foundation.* The wise builder knows the intelligence of building on a substantial foundation. Accordingly, Jesus used the foundations — the rock and the sand — to contrast the wise and foolish builders (Matt. 7:24-27). One used common sense, the other did not. To build on the rock one must accept Christ

and build on what he has commanded. To disobey is to put the structure of your life on the sand.

4. *Looking into a mirror.* "For if any be a hearer of the word, and not a doer, he is like unto a man beholding his natural face in a glass [mirror]: For he beholdeth himself, and goeth his way, and straightway forgetteth what manner of man he was" (Jas. 1:23,24). It makes no sense to look into a mirror and behold the blotches and disfigurements and do nothing about it. The Lord has used this sound, perceptible illustration to show the uselessness of hearing the Word and not obeying it. The Bible is the mirror for the soul, and only he who looks into it and sees himself as he is and *obeys* shall be blessed (Jas. 1:25).

5. *Saying and not doing.* "If a brother or sister be naked, and destitute of daily food, and one of you say unto them, Depart in peace, be ye warmed and filled; notwithstanding ye give them not those things which are needful to the body; what doth it profit" (Jas. 2:16)? Once again the Holy Spirit has appealed to sanity to enforce a point — the unreasonableness of faith without works. So in Jas. 2:14 we read: "What doth it profit, my brethren, though a man say he hath faith, and have not works? can faith save him?" No! for "by works a man is justified, and not by faith only" (Jas. 2:24). A faith that lacks works is as dead as a corpse (Jas. 2:26). Under point 4 we have seen that *hearing and not doing* is vain (Jas. 1:22); and now under this point we see that *saying and not doing* is also vain. The great sensible word in God's religion is *DO*.

6. *Prove your religion.* Common sense demands proof in the various affairs of life. This is why doctors take X-rays and run tests in laboratories; why a company employs a CPA to check its records; and why an individual hires a lawyer to examine the title of his property. And it is even more rational

for one to seek proof of his religion, for more is involved (Mk. 8:36-37).

Nothing makes more sense than this injunction: "Beloved, believe not every spirit, but try [prove] the spirits whether they are of God: because many false prophets are gone out into the world" (I Jno. 4:1). The Bereans were commended for exercising this kind of discernment and perception by comparing what they heard with what they read in the Scriptures (Acts 17:11). The Holy Spirit has given the Scriptures (II Pet. 1:21), and as we read them our human spirit tells uf if we have done them — thus the joint testimony of the two spirits, Holy Spirit and human spirit, proves that we are the children of God (Rom. 8:16). This way we know (I Jno. 2:3).

7. *The production of fruit.* Jesus used the Parable of the Sower in a call to reason (Matt. 13:3-5). As it is sensible in the material world, so it is in the spiritual world. It gives three things essential to the production of fruit: (1) a sower, (2) seed, and (3) proper soil. To expect gospel fruit without sowing the seed — teaching or preaching the word, Lk. 8:11 — violates common sense. No one expects fruit in the physical world without a planting, and neither should we in the spiritual world (Rom. 10:13,14). Every farmer knows that soils make a difference, and so do human hearts. Oftentimes the unproduction is not the fault of the farmer or the seed — but the soil; similarly, the lack of a gospel harvest may not be the fault of the teacher or the Word — but the heart of man (Matt. 13:15).

8. *Sowing and reaping.* "For whatsoever a man soweth, that shall he also reap" (Gal. 6:7). No one questions the rationality of this statement. You would believe it, if it were not in the Bible, if you saw it printed on the side of a barn. For it is sensible, and if it is rational materially, then does it not make just as much sense spiritually? Sow wheat and you reap wheat; sow oats and reap oats. Also, sow human isms

and you reap human churches; but if you sow the unadulterated word of God (Lk. 8:11), you shall reap the true, undenominational church of the Bible (Acts 2:36-47). Also, if you sow to the flesh, you shall reap corruption; but if you sow to the Spirit, you shall reap everlasting life (Gal. 6:8).

9. *The importance of today.* "But exhort one another daily, while it is called To-day; lest any of you be hardened through the deceitfulness of sin" (Heb. 3:13). The practicality of *today* is not questioned (Jas. 4:13,14). Procrastination is not a sound way to live. Tied to the post of postponement, you can never travel the road of success, materially or spiritually.

> Time was is past, thou canst not recall;
> Time is thou hast: employ the portion small;
> Time future is not, and may never be.
> Time present is the only time for thee.
> — Charles Edwards

10. *Take heed lest you fall.* "Wherefore let him that thinketh he standeth take heed lest he fall" (I Cor. 10:12). Taking heed to avoid falling makes sense to the derrick man on an oil rig; and so does it to the steel worker in constructing a skyscraper. And it is' even more vital religiously for more is involved. Paul's sounding this warning is proof that a child of God can fall; if he cannot, it would be senseless to warn him of falling. Read Jno. 15:3, Heb. 3:12 and Gal. 5:4.

11. *Let your light shine.* "Neither do men light a candle and put it under a bushel, but on a candlestick; and it giveth light unto all that are in the house" (Matt. 5:15). This is logical. It would be ridiculous to light a candle and then cover it to keep it from shining. Here Jesus used this illustration in a solicitation to His people to think. They are the light of the world and as such have the duty to shine before the world (Matt. 5:14,16). To hide themselves under some bushel would obstruct their light and do nothing to alleviate the world's

darkness. So do not pull down over your light a bushel of pride, or worldiness, or self-interest, or covetousness, or absenteeism, or human doctrine or anything else contrary to Christ. You were lighted to shine.

12. *Worthless salt.* "Ye are the salt of the earth: but if the salt have lost his savor, wherewith shall it be salted? it is thenceforth good for nothing, but to be cast out, and to be trodden under foot of man" (Matt. 5:13). We have a practical, sensible Jesus; thus His voice wrang with sensible truths with practical applications. When salt loses its distinctive quality, it is no longer able to function in its designated field and consequently loses its value. What is true of salt is true of disciples. Salt is to season food, and the disciple is to season society and save it from a stale and decaying state. If this makes sense, then it is sensible that each ask, "What kind of salt am I?"

13. *Restrain your tongue from evil.* "For he that will love life, and see good days, let him refrain his tongue from evil, and his lips that they speak no guile" (I Pet. 3:10). This is another sample of common sense religion. The need of it is evident on every hand. The tongue is not the eye, but it has provoked the eye to shed an ocean of tears; it is not the cheek, but it has blushed the cheek a million times; it is not the foot, but it has overworked the foot in endless steps to peddle gossip. The tongue — that little organ affects the other organs and all facets of our society. For the good of the world and your own happiness, try to control it (Jas. 3:2-8). If this is not common sense religion, surely there is none!

14. *Better to be condemned for right than wrong.* "For it is better, if the will of God be so, that ye suffer for well doing, than for evil doing" (I Pet. 3:17). This is an intelligent appraisal of human responsibility. No matter what you do, you will be criticized; so you cannot allow that to influence you to quit or change from right to wrong. Duty is to continue, the

world must keep on turning. Do right and let the attacks come; and try to grow a skin thick enough to withstand them.

15. *Smarter with age.* "Days should speak, and multitude of years should teach wisdom" (Job 32:7). *Should* but not always, for gray hair is no substitute for gray matter; but if the intellect is there, the experiences of age add to wisdom. Once again the common sense of God's religion is evident in that He legislated that the first requirement of a bishop demands that he be an elder, an older person (Tit. 1:5-7).

16. *A condition of eating.* "This we commanded you, that if any would not work, neither should he eat" (II Thess. 3:10). Of course, this refers to those who can work. Our world is one of work; and to think that we can have without working defies nature and observation. ". . . labour . . . that he may have" (Eph. 4:28) is the smart law of God. And if *nobody! nobody!* worked, we would soon see how smart this law really is. Being a command of God, work is a part of our religion; to refuse, violates it (Gen. 3:19). This is more proof of the sensibleness that characterizes the commands of God. All of His teachings have a special utility and are for the good of man.

17. *Duties to two distinct authorities.* "Render therefore unto Caesar the things which are Caesar's; and unto God the things that are God's" (Matt. 22:21). Nothing can be wiser and simpler than Christ's distinction between civil and divine authorities and His teaching on man's responsibility to each. Being subjects of a civil government — Caesar — it is only right that citizens obey their nation's harmonious laws and pay taxes to its support. God foresaw the need of civil government and thus ordained it for society's good (Rom. 13:1-7). His appointment of it carries the duty that Christians give tribute, custom, fear and honor to the officials of government.

Jesus also used this occasion to charge man with his duty to

God, which self-evidently comes first (Matt. 6:33). Church and state can exist together without conflict, each recognizing the role of the other and cooperating for the good of the community. Religion should respect the rights of Caesar, and Caesar should respect the conscience of religion. A community would be in a sad plight without either. This is unquestionably sensible.

18. *The answer of a good conscience.* "The like figure whereunto *even* baptism doth also now save us, (not the putting away of the filth of the flesh, but the answer of a good conscience toward God,) by the resurrection of Jesus Christ" (I Pet. 3:21). It is God's plan for man's conscience to answer to or respond to God's commandments for its cleansing and assurance. In this verse it answers to the command to be baptized, but the principle is true of all other divine commandments.

It makes no sense at all to say, "Let your conscience be your guide," if that conscience is untaught and unguided by the word of God. It would free a man from God's teachings and allow him to be his own god and to follow anything he thinks is right: to throw the children as sacrifices into the river that is worshiped, and to allow the cows as sacred creatures to roam the streets. Paul maintained a good conscience (Acts 23:1), but it was not enough — he went against Christ (Acts 26:9). You do not have to belong to the intelligentsia to see that for conscience to be a safe guide it must be governed by truth. Common sense tells us that.

In our complex society in which human frailty often succumbs, the clear conscience is an absolute requirement of spiritual and physical health. The condemning conscience, however, demands a cure that is deeper than what psychiatry can touch. The patient needs to obey God for forgiveness, take Him at His word that pardon has been granted, and then leave it behind (Phil. 3:13,14).

Shakespeare gave recognition to this sensible approach to one of life's most distressing problems. In Act V of Macbeth, the question arose as to who should treat Lady Macbeth's ailment. A physician was brought in, but listen to his opinion:

> This distress is beyond my practice.
> Foul whisperings are abroad!
> Unnatural deeds do breed unnatural troubles;
> Infected minds to their deaf pillows will
>   discharge their secrets.
> More needs she the Divine than the physician.
> God, God forgive us all.

CONCLUSION

The foregoing eighteen Scriptures — a few of many — show the unequivocal rationalism and depth of the divinely given religion.

REVIEW EXERCISE

1. What illustration did the Lord give to show that a person must be connected to Him? ....
   ....

2. What are the two foundations on which a person may build his life?
   (1) .... (2) ....

3. What illustration did James give to show the uselessness of hearing the Word and not obeying it? ....
   ....

4. Why does it make sense to prove your religion? ....
   ....

5. Why were the Bereans commended? ....

6. What three conditions are essential to the production of gospel fruit?

    (1) .... (2) ....

    (3) ....

7. What should we expect from sowing? ....
8. Why did Paul command the Christian to "take heed lest he fall?"

    ....

9. What illustration did Jesus use to show that if we lose our Christian qualities we are good for nothing? ....

    ....

10. Why is, "Let your conscience be your guide" insufficient? ....

    ....

11. (T or F) The Bible states that we can suffer for well doing.
12. (T or F) Years cannot help us to get any smarter.
13. (T or F) It is sinful to support people who are able to work and can work.
14. Thought for discussion: Discuss ways we can hide our light under a bushel.

XII

God's Appointment of Death Is Sensible

DEATH certainly works its havoc of indescribable miseries among the loved ones left behind: a broken relationship, a crushed heart, shattered plans, bitter loneliness and oftentimes financial hardships. But we must look beyond the loss of the bereaved to the benefits of the deceased. From that perspective we get a better view of the reasonableness of it.

If life is a rational thing, then so is death, for it is impossible to have one without the other. It is apparent that we cannot have death without life; and it is just as obvious that we cannot have life in this world without death. Suppose our world should operate free of death: that plant life should multiply and none ever dies; that animals should continuously come into the world and none ever leaves; that fowls should hatch in growing numbers and not a one perishes; that fishes should constantly reproduce but only to keep on living; and that human beings should multiply in countless numbers while nobody ever expires. We see that life would become an unbearable impossibility.

It is evident that life requires death. Every living thing — man, beast, plant, fowl and fish — has its day, and then must give way to death to make room for the coming of more life. Nature says this is right, for it is the only practical way that nature can operate.

There is the fable concerning a community that asked God to remove death from their midst. In this fictitious story God granted their request. As a result, the aged became older and older with no escape; the ill got sicker and weaker with no relief; the sufferers were wracked with ever increasing pain with no future except a more severe tomorrow; the mourners shed more and more tears with no hope to dry them. Life became a terrifying nightmare! An intolerable ordeal! Unable to bear life, they much preferred death. But they had to witness the rigors of a deathless society to really understand how desirable death can be. So they met and asked God to send death back to them. They had learned that death -- the commonly mistaken enemy of man — is actually a kind and considerate friend.

THE CAUSE OF DEATH

1. *Death naturally came after man was separated from the tree of life.* It stands to reason that when man lost accessibility to that which sustained perpetual youth, old age and death became the inborn results.

Man's first existence was in the Garden of Eden (Gen. 2:8). It was there that the first couple sinned (Gen. 3:1-6); and it was from there that they were expelled, lest they "take also of the tree of life, and eat, and live for ever" (Gen. 3:22). After this reference, we never find the tree of life mentioned again in the Bible until we come to the last book — Revelation — and there it is referred to in connection with another beautiful paradise which is heaven itself. There man may eat of it and live forever. The Lord has assured us, "To him that overcometh will I give to eat of the tree of life, which is in the midst of the paradise of God" (Rev. 2:7). So on the other side of the chasm of death there is a deathless state made possible by the presence of the tree of life.

Eternal life for man! But not in a state of sin and rebellion as would have been true, if man had not been driven from the Garden that contained the tree of life. Disjoined from the source of life, death had to follow; rejoined with it, eternal life has to ensue.

2. *So death came because of sin.* Paul states, "Wherefore, as by one man sin entered into the world, and death by sin; so death passed upon all men" (Rom. 5:12). It was sin that compelled God to oust man from the Garden and out of reach of the tree of life, which appointed death unto him. This spared man an eternal life on a sin-cursed earth. Death! But not extinction! Instead, a better life in a sinless, deathless realm. This is too necessary not to be true!

> He will not leave our treasures in the dust,
> For God is just. NECESSITATION!
> — Charles Carroll Albertson

Therefore, I insist:

> "Earth to earth, and dust to dust"
> Necessitates another must —
> It was not spoken of the soul.

THE NATURE OF MAN

1. *The very character and make-up of man sheds light on the common sense of death.* His dual nature — flesh and spirit — makes it possible for one portion of him to perish while the other part keeps on living. This truly puts death in a new perspective. The inspired apostle Paul states, "For which cause we faint not; but though our outward man perish, yet the inward man is renewed day by day" (II Cor. 4:16). One man perishes but the other is immortal. The seen man is temporal, but the unseen man is eternal (II Cor. 4:18).

Since man is a composite being with two qualities — a fleshly body with a spirit within — then life on earth is correctly described by Paul as, "Whilst we are at home in the body, we are absent from the Lord" (II Cor. 5:6). Then death, the opposite of life, is the spirit's leaving the body to go be with the Lord. Solomon's comment is pertinent: "Then shall the dust return to the earth as it was: and the spirit shall return unto God who gave it" (Eccl. 12:7). We see from the verse that two distinct natures are set free by death to go their destinies: one to the grave and the other to God. That is what death is, the dissolution of flesh and spirit. James brings out this thought in a very intelligible way: "For as the body without the spirit is dead" (Jas. 2:26). Way back in Genesis Moses presented this thought concerning Rachel's death: "And it came to pass, as her soul was in departing, (for she died,)" (Gen. 35:18). Departure! But not annihilation!

2. *Man's make-up will not allow annihilation.* Death does not end life — only changes the state of living. Hence, what we call death is only a new beginning — just a transition:

> There is no death! What seems so is transition:
> This life of mortal breath
> Is but a suburb of the life elysian,
> Whose portal we call death.
> — Henry Wadsworth Longfellow

DYING GIVES SENSE TO LIVING

1. *Life must continue after death or else there is no sense to living.* It is as the epitaph over a child's grave in an English churchyard puts it:

> If so early I am done for,
> What in the world was I begun for?

2. *If life does not continue after death,* then the Creator works and labors to no eternal accomplishment; and His plan is imperfect, unfulfilling and cuts man short of the hope of immortality implanted in his heart. Again I repeat: if death is extinction, then all of nature toils and travails to no avail.

Of all of earth's inhabitants, man stands out as a distinct and superior class. All others exist for his preservation and comfort. If death destroys him to never live again, then all is lost, forever lost. Vegetable life springs out of the earth and returns to the earth again. Animals are struck down by death with no hope of rising again. Day and night chase each other in a circle unbroken by the ages. Years revolve at a fast pace. Now if man — like vegetables and animals — perishes forever, what is gained by the whole operation? If this be true, man lives to no purpose, nature is a cruel miscarriage and God's plan of the universe is a nonsensical, disappointing failure.

3. *Thus life after death is a tribute to the mercy, wisdom and power of God.* Reason declares that it is no strain on His creative powers to provide life twice. For it is just as easy for the Creator to give life the second time as it was the first time. It is an accepted tenet of logic that *what has been can be.* Since life has been given once, it can be given twice.

And this brings us to another good reason for dying.

THESE BODIES ARE NOT SUITED TO ETERNITY

1. *Our earthly bodies are not adapted to an eternal habitation.* This is why they get old, become diseased and die. Since our bodies are not equipped for a spiritual abode, it is impossible for them to pass into heaven. Paul affirms this: "Now this I say, brethren, that flesh and blood cannot inherit the kingdom of God; neither doth corruption inherit incorruption" (I Cor. 15:50). This is intelligible.

2. *So in order to effect God's plan, it is necessary for man to die.* Paul uses a sensible fact from nature, that of sowing seed, to prove it: "But some man will say, How are the dead raised up? and with what body do they come? Thou fool, that which thou sowest is not quickened, except it die: And that

which thou sowest, thou sowest not that body that shall be, but bare grain, it may chance of wheat, or of some other grain" (I Cor. 15:35-37).

If the grain of wheat can die that the life within it be clothed with another grain, then I shall not doubt that when this body dies God has the power to clothe my spirit with a new body, adapted to an everlasting existence.

> Why should you be forlorn? Death
> only husks the corn.
> Why should you fear to meet the
> thresher of the wheat?
> — Maltbie D. Babcock

Concerning God's wise and judicious plan for this new body, the Bible states: "But God giveth it a body as it hath pleased him, and to every seed his own body" (I Cor. 15:38). "Who shall change our vile body, that it may be fashioned like unto his own glorious body, according to the working whereby he is able even to subdue all things unto himself" (Phil. 3:21). "It is sown in corruption, it is raised in incorruption. It is sown in weakness, it is raised in power; it is sown a natural body, it is raised a spiritual body (I Cor. 15:42-44).

3. *Let us bear in mind that a move from one house to another does not end the life of the tenant.* When this old house — this body — shall have broken down, man shall be given a fairer dwelling, made for eternity (II Cor. 5:1).

> This body is my house — it is not I;
> Herein I sojourn till, in some far sky,
> I lease a fairer dwelling, built to last
> Till all the carpentry of time is past.
> (In a new house away from) this lone star,
> What shall I care where these poor timbers are?

God's Appointment of Death   121

> What, though the crumbling walls turn dust and loam —
> I shall have left them for a larger home.
>
> — Frederick Lawrence Knowles

This victory is possible "through our Lord Jesus Christ" (I Cor. 15:57). For He is "the resurrection and the life," the power that enables those who are dead to live (Jno. 11:25).

GO HOME WHEN SCHOOL IS OUT

Inasmuch as this life is a time of preparation or schooling, then it is only natural that we go home when school is out. "Prepare to meet thy God" (Amos 4:12) gives direction and gratification to living; and when this is done, the homecoming is a joyous experience.

> Why be afraid of death as though your
> life were breath!
> Death but anoints your eyes with clay.
> O glad surprise!
>
> Why should it be a wrench to leave
> your wooden bench,
> Why not with happy shout run home
> when school is out?
>
> Maltbie D. Babcock

APPROACH DEATH WITH HOPE

1. *It is heartening to observe some of the strong characters in the Bible* who saw death disguised as a blessing:

Job: "For I know that my Redeemer liveth, and that he shall stand at the latter day upon the earth: And though after my skin worms destroy this body, yet in my flesh shall I see God" (Job 19:25,26).

David: "Yea, though I walk through the valley of the shadow of death, I will fear no evil . . . Surely goodness and mercy shall follow me all the days of my life: and I will dwell in the house of the Lord for ever" (Psa. 23:4-6).

Solomon: "Man goeth to his long home, and the mourners go about the streets" (Eccl. 12:5).

Paul: "For I am now ready to be offered, and the time of my departure is at hand. I have fought a good fight, I have finished my course, I have kept the faith: Henceforth there is laid up for me a crown of righteousness, which the Lord, the righteous judge, shall give me at that day: and not to me only, but unto all them also that love his appearing" (II Tim. 4:6-8).

2. *Because of faith and obedience we can have the blessed assurance* so eloquently set to lines by William Cullen Bryant in *Thanatopsis:*

> So live that, when thy summons comes to join
> The innumerable caravan which moves
> To that mysterious realm where each shall take
> His chamber in the silent halls of death,
> Thou go not like the quarry slave at night
> Scourged to his dungeon; but, sustained and soothed
> By an unfaltering trust, approach thy grave
> Like one who wraps the drapery of his couch
> About him and lies down to pleasant dreams.

REVIEW EXERCISE

1. Why does life require death?.......................................
2. What brought on the natural death of man after he was driven from the Garden of Eden? ....
3. How did Paul correctly describe life on earth? ....
   ....

4. What compelled God to oust man from the Garden of Eden?

   ....

5. Why is it that death cannot annihilate man?........................

   ....

6. Why is it "that flesh and blood cannot inherit the kingdom of God?"

   ....

7. What did Paul use a grain of seed to illustrate?......................

   ....

8. What kind of body is man to be given in heaven?....................

   ....

9. (T or F) The paradise of God contains the tree of life.
10. (T or F) No person can die and live at the same time.
11. Thought for discussion: If man does not live again, God's whole plan would end in failure.
12. Thought for discussion: It is no harder for God to give life the second time than it was the first time.

XIII

The Judgment Makes Sense

IN the previous chapter we studied the common sense of death. Now it is highly appropriate that we consider the sensibleness of the judgment.

> And as it is appointed unto men once to die, but after this the judgment.
>
> — Hebrews 9:27

Man through the ages has borne witness to the expectancy and usefulness of a final judgment. There is nothing unreasonable about it. Everything has its price. We have been given life but at the price of accounting for it. This is plausible.

Wherever you go in all the world you will find an inward conviction of the coming judgment day. Traverse the nominal Christian lands; or enter the bewildering cities of idolatry; or visit the wandering tribes; go to the most enlightened or to the most superstitious — and you will find in man "a certain fearful looking for a judgment" (Heb. 10:27). The diversity of expectations merely confirms that the common sense of all peoples supports the rationality of an accounting of this life.

THE JUDGMENT DAY

1. *Such a day is often spoken of in the Bible:*

(1) "The judgment of the great day" (Jude 6).

(2) The "revelation of the righteous judgment of God" (Rom. 2:5).

(3) Shall occur at the second coming of Christ and the end

of the world (Matt. 24:3; 25:31; II Pet. 3:10-14).

(4) All nations (Matt. 25:32), all people (Heb. 12:23), the small and the great (Rev. 20:12), the righteous and the wicked (Eccl. 3:17), the living and the dead (II Tim. 4:1), shall be there.

(5) Christ shall be acknowledged, even by those who denied Him on earth (Rom. 14:10,11).

(6) The books shall be the standard of judgment (Rev. 20:12).

(7) Our words shall be brought up (Matt. 12:36,37); so shall our deeds (Rom. 2:6).

(8) Even the secret things shall be judged (Rom. 2:16).

(9) A day of reward for the righteous (II Tim. 4:8); a day of perdition for ungodly men (II Pet. 3:7).

(10) Its certainty should be a motive to repent (Acts 17:30, 31), to watch and pray (Mk. 12:33), and to labor for acceptance (II Cor. 5:9,10).

JUSTICE DEMANDS THE JUDGMENT

1. *The judgment is essential to the triumph of justice.* How often it is said, if there is a God why is our world filled with suffering? Why does death hold all humanity in its grip? Why does the crook prosper off the earnings of honest people? Why does the innocent suffer and the criminal goes free? Is there no justice to be meted out to man?

2. It is apparent, therefore, that the judgment day is *necessary for God to vindicate His character* before angels and men as the God of fair treatment. How could He do otherwise than bless the good and condemn the evil?

3. *A day of reckoning is for the good of man and to the*

glory of God. The inventor of a gasoline engine is glorified if it is properly governed and made useful. Likewise, God's honor and man's happiness require that the Creator govern man in a manner adapted to his capacities, which means that God rule man in a style that conforms to man's volition and freedom of choice (Josh. 24:15). This freedom of choice enables man to follow righteousness or unrighteousness. And the best means to influence man to voluntarily follow the right course is to have the judgment in which the rewards are large and the penalties severe.

This principle is the basis of the criminal laws in all nations. But God's administration over human activity is wiser, more redressing and compensative than man's government. Oftentimes in a nation's management of human affairs, justice is so perverted that instead of rewarding the hard-working, thrifty, law-abiding citizen, he is actually penalized, while the indolent, irresponsible, law-breaking citizen is favored and blessed.

A nation brings dishonor upon itself by allowing its law-breakers to go unpunished. Logical thinking tells us that if God permitted this, He would be subject to the same criticism.

What would be the state of man on earth, if there were no courts and no one had to face judgment in court? Horrifying! God knew this and this is why He ordained civil government (Rom. 13:1-7). The laws are a necessity, but why have civil laws without civil courts? The courts with their judgments are needed to deal with offenders. Likewise, God has given laws to man. But why have the laws if we have not the judgment? So the final judgment is a necessary and reasonable thing. It is called "the righteous judgment of God" (II Thess. 1:5).

4. *A final judgment is needed to right some wrongs that*

are never righted in this life. On earth it rains on the just and the unjust (Matt. 5:45). While it is true that people usually suffer to some extent in this life for the sins they commit, it is also true that the perpetrator of evil often gets by with it so far as we can see. But, of course, his evil forges a rod that beats him when we are not looking. Anyway, fairness requires that the books be better balanced.

Relative to this thought, it is reputed that Justice Gray of the Supreme Court, when he was a judge in a lower court, said to a man who escaped conviction on a technicality: "I know that you are guilty and you know it, and I wish you to remember that one day you will stand before a better and wiser judge, and that there you will be dealt with according to justice and not according to some technicality of law."

5. *It is sensible that doors are open to some while those same doors are closed to others.* Why are some people allowed to enter the stadium, the coliseum and the theater, while others are shut out? Because of conditions which involve preparation. Some buy tickets. Some do not. Nobody ever questions the rationality of a little examination at the gate. Mankind says it is right and fair.

So do the Scriptures. The lesson is clear from the Parable of the Ten Virgins (Matt. 25:1-13). All had been invited to the marriage, all expected to enter, but only those who made the necessary preparation — "took oil in their vessels with their lamps" — were permitted to enter. That is not unreasonable. Let us remember that the bridegroom in the parable represents Jesus who *can* say, "I know you not," and who *can* shut the door that shall leave you on either the inside or outside of it. So where you stand forever when it is closed is determined by the preparation or lack of it that you now make. For where the judgment finds you, there eternity shall leave you.

6. *It makes sense that we be examined at the borderline as we cross into a foreign country.* Many of us have been examined at the custom house. The officers said something like this: "Do you have any contraband goods?" The usual reply was: "I don't think so." "That may be true," said the officers, "but we cannot let you pass without examination. Permit us to examine you." There is a great, practical lesson for us in this everyday, sensible procedure at the border. We are all travelers to an eternal kingdom that does not permit the entrance of any contraband goods. From Isaiah's prophecy we learn that the unclean cannot even travel the way that leads there: "And a highway shall be there, and a way, and it shall be called The way of holiness; the unclean shall not pass over it; but it shall be for those: the wayfaring men, though fools, shall not err therein" (Isa. 35:8). The unclean have no "inheritance in the kingdom of Christ and of God" (Eph. 5:5; Gal. 5:19-21; I Jno. 3:15). It would be a violation of mercy to the righteous to allow the evil to enter heaven and defile it. The wicked have done too much harm on earth to allow them to enter heaven and ruin it. You see, heaven is a place "where the wicked cease from troubling; and there the weary be at rest" (Job. 3:17). It would not make sense to permit those who have troubled this earth to enter heaven and disquiet it.

7. *It is fair and reasonable that we look to the one we serve for wages.* If we have served Satan, then it is right that we look to him for the pay-off; but if we have served God, it is sensible that we expect of Him the reward. This the Bible teaches: "For the wages of sin is death; but the gift of God is eternal life through Jesus Christ our Lord" (Rom. 6:23). Hence, a judgment that hands out the wages or rewards is nothing but fair; and if it is fair of this life, it is fair of the next one.

THE RIGHTEOUS JUDGE

I am especially thankful that the Lord is going to be the judge. It would unnerve me to think that some person or jury of persons should hand down the decisions on that last day. Man is too unknowledgeable, unmerciful, unfair and biased to sit in that role to suit me. I prefer to leave my destiny in the hands of Him who does all things wisely, understandably and mercifully. I am glad that "the righteous judge" Jesus shall execute the judgment (Matt. 25:31,32).

1. *The Divine Judge has all the facts.* "The eyes of the Lord are in every place, beholding the evil and the good" (Prov. 15:3). "All things are naked and opened unto the eyes of him with whom we have to do" (Heb. 4:13).

Too frequent man is ignorant of the facts. A fragment of knowledge is apt to be deceptive. How little we know of what goes on in the heart of the other person. We know some things about another because of his words and deeds (Matt. 12:33, 34), unless the words are feigned and the deeds are hypocritical. But it is quite possible for us to miss the real motive and the extenuating circumstances involved. Too often we judge according to appearances which Jesus prohibits (Jno. 7:24). An outward judgment would have accepted the Pharisees, for they were beautiful on the outside but rotten within (Matt. 23:28). However, God's eyes see deeper. "For the Lord seeth not as man seeth; for man looketh on the outward appearance, but the Lord looketh on the heart" (I Sam. 16:7).

2. *This Judge is impartial and unbiased.* He is "no respecter of persons" (Acts 10:34). Race, color, education, social standing, money or politics cannot influence His decisions.

Neither will our forgiven sins prejudice Him against us. Some experts assert that absolute and complete *forgetting* is not possible for the human mind. If so, then long-passed incidents may crop up and unintentionally affect judgments and relationships pertaining to any person involved in one's memory. This would make infallible judgments for man an impossibility. But with the Lord it is different. He can forgive; and when He forgives, He remembers the sin no more forever (Heb. 8:12). This assures a kinder and truer judgment than man can render.

3. The justice of our Judge is seen in that *He requires of each only in keeping with one's ability.* This is evident from the Parable of the Talents (Matt. 25:14-30). The one talent man was obligated to gain one talent; the two talent man, two; and the five talent man, five. "To whom men have committed much, of him they will ask the more" (Lk. 12:48). This makes sense.

4. Lest we misunderstand God, we need to learn that *He, like nature, has two sides, a side that is pleasant and a side that is stern.* In nature: the gentle breezes are sometimes displaced by a destructive tornado; the rippling of shallow waters sometimes turn into a roaring flood; and the bloom and delicacy of the rose is occasionally marred by the pricks from its thorns. This suggests that the God of nature who is filled with compassion is also strict. We remember that the Bible declares that "it is a fearful thing to fall into the hands of the living God" (Heb. 10:31).

Nature has her times of judgment, which are followed by the destruction of the troublesome and worthless. This enforces on our minds the thought that while God abounds in goodness and mercy, He does require us to stand some day before his judgment bar and face His teachings.

TIME OF JUDGMENT IS UNKNOWN TO MAN

No man knows when the world will end and the judgment

day will come: "no man, no, not the angels which are in heaven, neither the Son, but the Father" (Mk. 13:32). Yet the self-appointed prophets keep on setting the dates. But the Bible says they do not know. A glaringly incongruous way to handle the Bible!

Rather than know the date of the Lord's return and the final judgment, it is much wiser for man to live in a daily state of watchfulness and readiness (Matt. 24:42-44).

REVIEW EXERCISE

1. We have been given life at the price of ....
2. Wherever you go you find in man "a certain fearful looking ....
  .... "
3. Why does God's rulership of man demand the judgment? ....
  ....
4. Why are doors open to some and closed to others? ....
  ....
5. Explain that it makes sense for us to be examined before being permitted to enter a foreign country.................................
  ....
6. Why do we prefer to have the Lord instead of man to judge us?
  ....
7. How much will the Lord require of us at the judgment? ....
  ....
8. (T or F) Christ shall not be acknowledged at the judgment by those who denied Him on earth.
9. (T or F) The judgment is called righteous.

10. (T or F) The judgment is essential to the triumph of justice.
11. Question for discussion: How could God's character permit Him to do otherwise than bless the good and condemn the evil?
12. Thought for discussion: Since the books shall be the standard of judgment, then nothing should come up that we are not expecting.